The Recipe for Simple Business Improvement

Also available from ASQ Quality Press:

Making Change Work: Practical Tools for Overcoming Human Resistance to Change
Brien Palmer

Transformational Leadership: Creating Organizations of Meaning
Stephen Hacker and Tammy Roberts

The Executive Guide to Improvement and Change
G. Dennis Beecroft, Grace L. Duffy, and John W. Moran

From Quality to Business Excellence: A Systems Approach to Management
Charles Cobb

The Change Agent's Guide to Radical Improvement
Ken Miller

The Change Agents' Handbook: A Survival Guide for Quality Improvement Champions
David W. Hutton

Strategic Navigation: A Systems Approach to Business Strategy
H. William Dettmer

Principles and Practices of Organizational Performance Excellence
Thomas J. Cartin

From Baldrige to the Bottom Line: A Road Map for Organizational Change and Improvement
David W. Hutton

Customer Centered Six Sigma: Linking Customers, Process Improvement, and Financial Results
Earl Naumann and Steven H. Hoisington

The Certified Quality Manager Handbook, Second Edition
Duke Okes and Russell T. Westcott, editors

To request a complimentary catalog of ASQ Quality Press publications, call (800) 248-1946, or visit our bookstore at http://www.asq.org.

The Recipe for Simple Business Improvement

David W. Till

ASQ Quality Press
Milwaukee, Wisconsin

American Society for Quality, Quality Press, Milwaukee 53203
© 2004 by David W. Till
All rights reserved. Published 2003
Printed in the United States of America

12 11 10 09 08 07 06 05 04 03   5 4 3 2 1

Library of Congress Cataloging-in-Publication Data

Till, David W., 1949–
 The recipe for simple business improvement / David W. Till.
  p. cm.
 Includes bibliographical references and index.
 ISBN 0-87389-609-2 (Hardcover, case bound : alk. paper)
 1. Reengineering (Management). 2. Total quality management. 3.
Business planning. 4. Leadership. 5. Industrial management. I. Title.

HD58.87.T55 2003
658.4'063—dc22   2003022148

ISBN 0-87389-609-2

Publisher: William A. Tony
Acquisitions Editor: Annemieke Hytinen
Project Editor: Paul O'Mara
Production Administrator: Barbara Mitrovic
Special Marketing Representative: David Luth

ASQ Mission: The American Society for Quality advances individual,
organizational, and community excellence worldwide through learning,
quality improvement, and knowledge exchange.

Attention Bookstores, Wholesalers, Schools, and Corporations: ASQ Quality
Press books, videotapes, audiotapes, and software are available at quantity
discounts with bulk purchases for business, educational, or instructional use.
For information, please contact ASQ Quality Press at 800-248-1946, or write to
ASQ Quality Press, P.O. Box 3005, Milwaukee, WI 53201-3005.

To place orders or to request a free copy of the ASQ Quality Press Publications
Catalog, including ASQ membership information, call 800-248-1946. Visit our
Web site at www.asq.org or http://qualitypress.asq.org.

 Printed on acid-free paper

Quality Press
600 N. Plankinton Avenue
Milwaukee, Wisconsin 53203
Call toll free 800-248-1946
Fax 414-272-1734
www.asq.org
http://qualitypress.asq.org
http://standardsgroup.asq.org
E-mail: authors@asq.org

This book is dedicated to my wife, Toni.
She has been my inspiration throughout my life.
This book was written as a result of her prompting.

Table of Contents

List of Figures and Tables

Preface

Continuous improvement programs are certainly not new. They have evolved from the approaches that W. Edwards Deming used to help Japanese businesses recover after World War II. The various improvement programs are called many different names, including total quality management (TQM), reengineering, and Six Sigma.

There are many examples that prove these programs to be successful. However, there are also many stories of companies that have attempted to implement business improvement programs and failed.

My experience indicates that implementing a successful quality improvement program is like baking a cake. Not only are all of the ingredients essential for success, but so is the sequence in which they are put together and the timing of when each ingredient is added. The reason some businesses fail in implementation is that the recipe is not correctly applied. Either some ingredients are missing or the timing is off, so the reaction fails to activate business improvement as needed.

The Recipe for Simple Business Improvement lays out an effective, uncomplicated path that can be followed by any organization, small or large, to bring about significant business improvement. This book will prove useful to small-business owners and managers, who need a business improvement process that is simple to apply, easy on the budget, and geared for rapid results. It will also prove useful to senior leaders and functional managers of larger organizations. These leaders and managers will benefit from the uncomplicated approach that ensures alignment of projects with strategic direction and provides methods, such as the elimination of wasteful events, to maintain focus on important activities.

The Recipe for Simple Business Improvement is particularly suitable for organizations in which resources are limited or there is a desire to gain rapid improvement. This book will also prove valuable in organizations already pursuing programs such as Six Sigma. These organizations can use the book to ensure that the key ingredients or enablers are in place to ensure success and that projects being carried out are in alignment with strategic direction.

The opening section of the book provides a brief history of the development of continuous improvement. The approaches advocated by the modern gurus are outlined, and successful companies' stories are told. The invisible barrier to change that exists in every organization is introduced, and the application of the six key ingredients to overcome the barrier is defined.

The middle section of the book describes in detail the six key ingredients. This section will provide readers with the fundamental understanding of the basic building blocks that underpin all successful business improvement programs. The critical importance of the roles of leaders is emphasized, for without true leadership no program will be fully implemented or successful. Leaders also have the onerous task of setting the strategy for the business and then marshaling resources toward the business's goals and objectives. A three-pronged implementation plan is outlined that provides linkage between the strategy, the projects undertaken, and the skills needed for successful completion. Guidelines on training needed to accomplish projects are provided, along with methods to manage the teams and motivate involvement through reward and recognition.

Chapter 8 summarizes the book by depicting the fictitious account of the implementation of *The Recipe* in the *Little Brick Company*. Although this particular story is fictitious, it epitomizes my experience in applying the recipe for business improvement in the real world.

Finally all of the forms and worksheets used throughout are provided. These forms and worksheets can help readers to implement the process in their own work environment.

Acknowledgments

My wife Toni who was my frontline editor, reading and reviewing every page when first produced.

Gary Markle for advising me to read a couple of books about how to write and get published before I ever started writing. He saved me countless hours of wasted work.

The editor, Paul O'Mara, and Barbara Mitrovic of ASQ Quality Press whose input made this work so much better.

My agent Marissa Carter who gave so much advice and took away all of the other burdens associated with writing and publishing a book.

Introduction: Brief History of the Development of Continuous Improvement

MANY GURUS, ONE SYSTEM OF BELIEFS

The *Collins English Dictionary* defines a "guru" as a spiritual teacher.[1] So who are the spiritual teachers of the art of continuous improvement? Who are the people who have spent a fair proportion of their lives preaching to anyone who would listen to them about the benefits and methodologies of improving business performance? Many earn a living in the field, but few carry the accolade of guru. Gurus are the authors that most other writers refer to in anything that is published on the topic.

The better known names are Deming, Joseph M. Juran, Philip B. Crosby, and Michael Hammer from the United States, Kaoru Ishikawa and Taiichi Ohno from Japan, and John S. Oakland from the United Kingdom—a sort of seven samurai of the business world. All of these authors have written extensively on the subject of business improvement.

Deming is credited with beginning the business revolution in Japan in the 1950s, which led to the dramatic increase in the quality of Japanese products that we continue to hear so much about today.[2] After the war, Deming went to Japan and developed the concept that says if a company improves quality, the following events occur:

- The company's costs decrease because of less rework, fewer mistakes, fewer delays, and better use of machine time and materials.

- Productivity improves in the company.

- The company captures the market with better quality and lower costs.

- The company stays in business.

- The company provides jobs and more jobs.

This concept links the strategic nature of the business to the role of improvement and to the two key goals of better satisfying customers' needs and reducing cost simultaneously.

As the result of Deming's work, companies such as Honda, Toyota, Canon, and Fuji slowly overhauled their giant corporations into the world-class businesses they are today. Deming's approach is steeped in the application of statistical techniques to systematically analyze and solve problems to reduce defects.

As part of the program to improve the knowledge of Japanese engineers, the Union of Japanese Scientists and Engineers (JUSE) also requested Juran's help. He made his first visit to Japan in 1954 and became closely involved in teaching Japanese management the techniques of quality improvement. In his book *Managerial Breakthrough,* Juran discusses the purpose of management, describes the individual steps that the manager must take to initiate or control change, and analyzes the significant issues implicit in the creation or prevention of change.[3] His approach starts with the proposition that all managerial activity is directed either at breaking through into new levels of performance (that is, breakthrough, or creation of change) or holding the resultant gains following breakthrough (that is, control or prevention of change). In his later work, Juran talks about three basic steps to progress: structured annual improvements combined with a sense of urgency, massive training programs, and upper management leadership.

Another guru, Crosby, is well known for his concept of *zero defects,* which he developed while he was a quality manager for the Pershing missile project prior to joining ITT as director of quality in 1965. In his book *The Eternally Successful Organization: The Art of Corporate Wellness,* Crosby makes the following observations:[4]

- People will take quality as seriously as the management takes it, no more.

- Integrity is unrelenting; it can't be achieved with short bursts of enthusiasm stemming from regret.

- Quality improvement needs to be thought of in terms of earnings per share. A well established process will double the amount of earnings per share.

- All the individuals in an organization need continual education concerning their roles in getting things done right the first time, and clear requirements on the changing scene within which they live and operate.

Ishikawa, the most sought after quality consultant in Japan, has worked with many major U.S. companies. His involvement with quality management commenced in 1949 when he started working with JUSE during its early involvement with Deming and Juran.[5] Deming credits Ishikawa with the accomplishment of formalizing the use of quality circles in Japan, a tool that is talked about and copied the world over. In addition, one of the most useful statistical tools—the cause-and-effect or fishbone diagram—is also known as the Ishikawa diagram after its originator.[6]

In chapter 6 of his book *What Is Total Quality Control?: The Japanese Way,* Ishikawa describes total quality control (TQC) as a thought revolution in management, the basics of which he states are:[7]

- If TQC is implemented companywide, it can contribute to the improvement of a company's corporate health and character.

- Quality assurance (QA) must be one of the major objectives of the company. QA must be the company's new management philosophy.

- Company leaders must set their eyes on long-term profits and put quality first.

- The company must abolish sectionalism.

- TQC is management with facts.

- TQC is management based on respect for humanity.

- Quality control (QC) is a discipline that combines knowledge with action.

The second Japanese member of the seven samurai, Taiichi Ohno is known as the father of lean manufacturing and worked with Eiji Toyoda to develop what is known today as the Toyota production method. In the book *The Machine That Changed the World,* James P. Womack, Daniel T. Jones, and Daniel Roos identify the principles of lean production as:[8]

- Teamwork

- Communication

- Efficient use of resources and elimination of waste

- Continuous improvement

The only British guru among the seven samurai is Oakland, the Exxon chemical professor of total quality management of the University of Bradford Management Centre. In the final chapter of his book *Total Quality Management,* Oakland discusses continuous improvement. He says, "To maintain a wave of interest in quality it is necessary to develop generations of managers who not only understand but are dedicated to the pursuit of never-ending improvement."[9] Oakland then gives the three basic principles for never-ending improvement:

1. Focus on the customer—the purpose of all work is to serve the customer better.

2. Understand the process—if there is one difference between management in the Far East and the West, it is that the Far East managers are closer to and more involved in the process than their counterparts in the West.

3. Involve the people—when people are treated like machines, work becomes uninteresting and unsatisfying. Under such conditions, it is impossible to expect quality services and reliable products.

The final guru of the seven, Michael Hammer, is the originator of the concept of reengineering. In their book *Reengineering the Corporation,* Hammer and James A. Champy state:

> Quality programs work within the framework of a company's existing processes and seek to enhance them by means of what the Japanese call kaizen or continual incremental improvement. The aim is to do what we already do only do it better. . . . Reengineering as we have seen seeks breakthrough not by enhancing existing processes, but by discarding them and replacing them with entirely new ones.[10]

Hammer and Champy advocate that the process of redesign should start with a clean sheet and not from a map of the existing process. Juran, however, advocated breakthrough back in 1954. Whether you start with a clean sheet or the existing map does not seem to matter. You have to know where you are and where you ultimately want to be if you are going to successfully make the transition. So, you need both to be able to move into action.

Deming, Juran, Crosby, Ishikawa, Ohno, Hammer, and Oakland have all contributed significantly to the knowledge about TQM and how to use it to improve business performance. However, my conclusion is that they are seven preachers basically talking about the same religion. They are all preaching that the route to long-term success for any organization is to concentrate on improving the quality of the processes that produce the products and provide the services of the enterprise. Each guru recommends a slightly different road map for companies to follow. Although the gurus' routes differ, they all have the same destination in mind and have similar milestones or markers that must be passed on the way. Those similar markers are:

- Top management must be committed.

- Improving quality must become a driving strategy.

- The organization must be systematic in its approach.

- Everyone must be educated and trained to make the change.

- Systematic measurement of results must be shared openly.

- The organization must develop teamwork and involve all members.

SUCCESSFUL COMPANIES' APPROACHES

Over the years, I have benchmarked and reviewed many companies' business improvement approaches. Here is a look at some of those approaches.

In 1988, A. Richard Shores, the quality manager of a division of Hewlett-Packard (HP), wrote a book called *Survival of the Fittest* in which he described HP's approach to total quality.[11] He indicated that HP had four essential functions:

- *Customer focus*—treating everything as a process and seeking feedback from customers about how to improve.

- *Management commitment*—clear business plan and goals and management review throughout the organization.

- *Total participation*—companywide involvement through quality teams.

- *Systematic analysis*—fact-based method that uses statistical tools.

In chapter 11, he described an approach to systematic process analysis:

U	Understand
S	Select
A	Analyze
PDCA	Plan–do–check–adopt

He explained that HP used this approach to systematically solve quality issues. He noted, "The process analysis method is known under many names: TQC cycle, Deming Wheel, or PDCA cycle. . . . The model begins by focusing on customer expectations and proceeds with an ordered set of process analysis tools."[12]

The Tennant Company, which Crosby described as having one of the best quality programs in the United States, has its story told in its publication *Quest for Quality* by Roger L. Hale.[13] Hale described the five key elements in the program:

1. Management commitment that starts at the top

2. Employee involvement in which 30 percent of the employees are involved at a time

3. Cooperative, nonadversarial worker/management relationships

4. Something in it for the people

5. Time, energy, and determination

Hale indicated that quality is a marathon not a sprint. It requires an uncompromising commitment by everyone, especially top management.

Union Carbide's quality program—*excellence through quality* (EQ)—is described by Stephen J. Will and S. Charles Zeynel in their article "The Senior Manager's Role in Quality Improvement."[14] They describe the process as a progression of five basic concepts:

- *Realism*—the company must see the current state of the business realistically.

- *Vision*—the company must see new possibilities in familiar things and create an image of the future that is better in specific ways than the present.

- *Flexibility*—even when the plan is complete, emerging forces in the environment and industry can always send the company back to the first step.

- *Commitment to continuous change*—if the company is truly going to start on the path that links the present to a better future, change must occur.

- *Hard work to effect the change*—as leaders in the quality effort, managers are a combination of coach, cheerleader, and captain of the team. As coaches, they plan the strategies, select the players, and monitor progress toward the goal. They emphasize training and development to promote continuous improvement for everyone in the organization. They cheer the team on by applauding and rewarding desirable behaviors and changes. But in this case, the leaders must also run the race. The leaders inspire and motivate by performing well and working personally to improve.

George H. Labovitz and Yu Sang Chang studied companies that had won the Deming Prize.[15] The objective of their research was to identify practices that were consistently evident in Deming prize winners but rare in other companies. In their article "Learn from the Best," they identified the following five traits:

1. *A plan for success*—the plan is well communicated throughout the company in a visual, readily understood manner.

2. *The executive role*—executives are required to seek out middle managers and solicit their input on quality improvement opportunities and goals.

3. *Keeping all customers satisfied*—the plan identifies and assigns specific tasks and responsibilities to virtually all departments and sections because the involvement of all parts of the company is required to achieve customer satisfaction.

4. *Striving for total involvement*—65 percent or more of employees are active in total quality efforts.

5. *Consistent training*—in contrast to the disconnected bursts of quality-related training common in many other corporate settings, the Deming Prize winners' investment in developing quality awareness and improvement skills is steady and ongoing.

The latest craze to hit the business improvement world is Six Sigma. Pioneered by Motorola in the mid 1980s and further refined through the '90s, major corporations such as GE and Allied Signal have used the technique as part of their growth and transformation strategies with tremendous success. In their book *The Six Sigma Way Team Fieldbook,* Peter S. Pande, Robert P. Neuman, and Roland R. Cavanagh describe how a Six Sigma organization embraces six essential themes:[16]

1. *A genuine focus on the customer*—this focus is backed by an attitude that puts the customers' needs first and by systems and strategies that tie the business to the voice of the customer.

2. *Data- and fact-driven management*—effective management systems track both results and outcomes (the *Y*s) and process, input, and other predictive factors (the *X*s).

3. *Process focus, management, and improvement* as an engine for growth and success. Processes in Six Sigma are documented, communicated, measured, and refined on an ongoing basis. They are also designed or redesigned at intervals to stay current with customer and business needs.

4. *Proactive management*—this type of management involves having habits and practices that anticipate problems and changes, applying facts and data, and questioning assumptions about goals and how the company does things.

5. *Boundaryless collaboration*—the cooperation between internal groups and external groups such as customers, suppliers, and supply chain partners.

6. *A drive for perfection, yet a tolerance for failure*—this duality gives people in a Six Sigma organization the freedom to test new approaches even while managing risks and learning from mistakes, thereby raising the bar of performance and customer satisfaction.

In Six Sigma programs, full-time resources called Black Belts are intensively trained for four weeks over a period of four months in the tools and techniques needed to run successful projects. The number of Black Belts in Six Sigma companies varies but is usually in the range of one Black Belt for every 50 to 100 employees. Supporting people on the teams are not full-time Six Sigma resources, but they do receive two weeks of training to reach the Green Belt level. Projects are tackled using the DMAIC method:

D   Define

M   Measure

A   Analyze

I   Improve

C   Control

The results obtained from such efforts are well documented. However, the implementation of such a program requires significant investments if the program is to be successful. In *The Six Sigma Way,* the example of GE Capital Services is given.[17] According to Pande, Neuman, and Cavanagh, this company invested $53 million and saved $53 million in 1996, invested $88 million and saved $261 million in 1997, and invested $98 million and saved $310 million in 1998. The returns are impressive, but not all companies have the resources to commit to such a program. Small companies will find it particularly difficult to allocate full-time bodies to the business improvement process. Training periods of four weeks are difficult to swallow as well.

The development of the approaches taken by the companies I described in this section (and others I reviewed) appears to be following a natural evolution. These approaches are progressively incorporating the teachings of all of the gurus.

WHY YOU DON'T HAVE TO WORRY ABOUT BEING AN EXPERT

The good news is that the methods work. The better news is that continuous improvement is not as complicated as some people present it. The best news is that you don't have to reinvent the wheel—you just get it rolling.

ENDNOTES

1. *Collins English Dictionary* (London: Collins, 2000).
2. W. Edwards Deming, *Out of the Crisis* (Cambridge: MIT, 1982).
3. Joseph M. Juran, *Managerial Breakthrough* (New York: McGraw-Hill, 1964).
4. Philip B. Crosby, *The Eternally Successful Organization: The Art of Corporate Wellness* (New York: McGraw-Hill, 1988).
5. Kaouri Ishikawa, *What Is Total Quality Control?: The Japanese Way* (New Jersey: Prentice Hall, 1985).
6. Ibid.
7. Ibid.
8. James P. Womack, Daniel T. Jones, and Daniel Roos, *The Machine That Changed the World: The Story of Lean Production* (New York: HarperCollins, 1991).
9. John S. Oakland, *Total Quality Management* (Oxford, England: Heinemann, 1989).
10. Michael Hammer and James A. Champy, *Reengineering the Corporation: A Manifesto for Business Revolution* (New York: Harper Business, 1991).
11. A. Richard Shores, *Survival of the Fittest* (Milwaukee: ASQC Quality Press, 1988).
12. Ibid.
13. Roger L. Hale, Douglas R. Hoelscher, and Ronald E. Kowal, *Quest for Quality: How One Company Put Theory to Work* (Minneapolis: Tennant Company, 1987).
14. Stephen J. Will, and S. Charles Zeynel, "The Senior Manager's Role in Quality Management," *Quality Progress* (January 1991): 66–68.

15. George H. Labovitz and Yu Sang Chang, "Learn from the Best," *Quality Progress* (May 1990): 87–89.
16. Peter S. Pande, Robert P. Neuman, and Roland R. Cavanagh, *The Six Sigma Way Team Fieldbook: An Implementation Guide for Process Improvement Teams* (New York: McGraw-Hill, 2000).
17. Ibid.

1

Why Improvement Doesn't "Just Happen"

THE REACTION THAT NEEDS TO OCCUR AND THE BARRIERS THAT HAVE TO BE BROKEN

The common advice of the gurus has been around since World War II. Why is it then that every company has not already successfully applied the gurus' methodologies and is operating today at a world-class level? Why have some companies not even started? Why have other companies been unable to get the seemingly simple methods going? Why can some divisions in a company successfully apply the methods but others are unable or unwilling to make it happen? These questions bothered me for most of my professional career. Then I recalled some of the teachings in my chemistry textbook *Comprehensive Chemistry* by John Hicks. Hicks said:

> The natural tendency of any system when left to itself is to assume the lowest possible energy state; this is seen in all branches of science and forms the basis of one of its greatest generalizations, the second law of thermodynamics.
>
> The way in which water flows to the lowest possible level, heat flows from a hotter body to a cooler one, gas diffuses throughout a vessel, and an electric charge flows from one point to another of lower potential are common examples of this universal tendency. It is not surprising therefore, to find that in all chemical reactions which proceed spontaneously that there is a loss of energy in the system. This raises the question of why all such reactions do not proceed with vigor and speed. . . .

The accepted explanation is that before two substances can combine together, these molecules must possess, at the moment of impact, at least a certain amount of energy known as the *energy of activation* of that reaction. Without this energy, the collision is unfruitful and no reaction occurs.[1]

This effect is described in Figure 1.1.

As I thought of Hicks's comments, I began to realize that the slow or failed implementation process I witnessed at many companies was the result of having to overcome an unseen barrier very similar to this activation energy. The barrier consisted of three parts:

- Failure to recognize the need and the gains that could be made

- Resistance to change and the attitude "the way we have always done it has proven okay in the past, so why change?"

- Lack of will to put in the effort to learn new skills and make a behavioral change

Like pushing a snowball up a hill, programs that were applied but failed to gain enough momentum to pass the activation barrier slowly crumbled and fell back to the starting position. This was particularly true when the programs were applied as the "flavor of the month" or were incomplete in their approach.

The first part of the barrier is the failure to recognize the need for change. In the current intensely competitive landscape, it appears that some senior managers still think their companies are immune to this competition. Although this mind-set is incomprehensible to most people, there are definitely some senior managers who think this way. I believe this mind-set is due to the fact that these senior managers are running the business from an

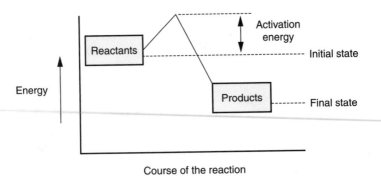

Figure 1.1 The energy of activation barrier.

operating perspective and not spending enough time reviewing the strategic issues of the business—what's happening with customers, competitors, markets, and technology.

When you read annual reports and look at the various committees that directors serve on, you rarely see a strategy committee, which is probably one of the most important areas the directors should be reviewing.

Not reviewing a company's strategic direction can have dire consequences. Consider, for example, a senior management team in a metals business in which I was involved. The metals division was the leader in its industry segment and had grown through acquisition over the previous five years. The senior managers became obsessed with outperforming their competitors, which the managers perceived as the larger folks in the industry in North America and Europe. The senior managers began to invest heavily in new product research and better equipment at their plants in an effort to give their customers better products at lower cost. All of their continuous improvement projects were aimed at internal cost reduction. They looked to Europe for their expansion and acquired one company as a foothold and were ready for the assault to buy out their beaten European competitors. However, the managers failed to look at what was happening with their customers, which were progressively moving to Asia in search of cheaper labor for assembly-type manufacturing processes. Suddenly, the senior managers found their home market had shrunk by 25 percent, and customers in a buyers' market forced prices down to the point at which the metals business was no longer making money. Despite all of the senior managers' cost-cutting efforts, the division was no longer able to grow where the market was. The metals business was forced to retrench and become a small North American player in the global market that it once led.

The second portion of the barrier is resistance to change. In many companies, the activities applied to start continuous improvement seemed themselves to increase the resistance to change in the participants. I saw a prime example of this in a manufacturing plant of a division that was losing money. The plant had long been the flagship facility, but now the plant manager was under pressure to cut costs to help the profitability of the division. Being responsible for the largest plant, he was expected to contribute more to the survival program. His boss was meeting with him twice a month and out of desperation he decided to start 10 teams to solve the plant's problems.

What the plant manager failed to realize was that with the limited resources he had and the fact that all his managers and supervisors were already working 10-hour days, he was just pushing them toward the breaking point. The whole workforce was totally resistant as a result of the overwhelming stress. After three months of this intense activity, his boss recommended to senior management that they fire the plant manager. I was asked by the president of the division to review the situation and see whether there was any alternative.

After a week's review at the plant, the plant manager and I ran a two-day seminar during which we defined a clear mission for the plant, defined the roles of the management team and the key supervisors, and brought the improvement process down to just three projects that were perfectly aligned with the mission. After just three months, the improvement teams reduced customer issues by 30 percent, reduced scrap by 25 percent, and cut costs by almost $1 million. In addition, the employee turnover rate began dropping as the stress level on the workforce was relieved.

The third part of the barrier is the lack of will to make the behavioral changes needed. My experience here is that most people are willing to change but lack the ability to coach themselves through it. How many times have you been on a training course, gone back to work, put the books on your bookcase, and then carried on behaving as if you'd never been away from your desk? It is essential that senior managers become the coaches for junior managers, who in turn become the coaches for supervisors, who in turn become the coaches for shop-floor workers.

Who can be the coaches for senior leaders? Look amongst yourselves. In every group of 10 people, there is usually one advocate, one naysayer, and eight people sitting on the fence. Let the advocate be your coach. Also search for expertise within your company's quality department.

WHY THE USUAL APPROACH OF HEAT AND PRESSURE LEADS TO CHAOS

There is continuous external pressure from customers who want more for less, shareholders who demand greater returns, competitors that continuously raise the bar, and governments that continuously add rules that have to be abided by. Because these forces turn up the heat and pressure on the leaders of the business, the leaders, in turn, often turn up the heat and pressure on the workforce.

Many people say there is a need for this "burning platform for change"; I would argue that it merely heats up the business and creates chaos unless there is a clear strategic direction that the workforce buys into and is focused to follow. This situation is shown in Figure 1.2.

Many managers do not know how to deal with this extra pressure other than to work longer hours and do more. Confounded by the conflicting roles of "keep doing what you're doing" and "make changes, reduce cost, and increase speed," many workers feel stressed and rapidly burn out.

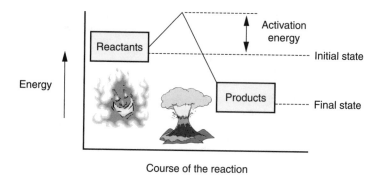

Figure 1.2   The usual approach of heat and pressure.

The key here is that it's essential to be sure everyone is working on and trying to improve the important tasks. It's also essential to *stop* doing those tasks that don't really count in order to make time for what's important. If no effort is made to reduce the unnecessary work and free up time for people to work on improvement, the only way for teams to function is by working extra hours, which creates further resistance to the improvement process.

HOW THE REACTION CAN BE CATALYZED TO REDUCE THE ENERGY NEEDED FOR SUCCESS

In *Comprehensive Chemistry,* Hicks talks about the use of a catalyst to accelerate a reaction. As Figure 1.3 shows, a catalyst can increase the rate of a reaction by providing an alternative route, each stage of which has a lower activation energy than the uncatalyzed reaction. Therefore, the catalyzed reaction is relatively fast.

An analogy is a person trying to get from one point to another in a mountainous area. The person will find it easier to travel the roundabout route over several small peaks rather than the direct route over the large mountain standing directly between the two points.

I began to realize that you could initiate a catalyzed reaction in a quality program. Like baking a cake, there was a certain recipe for success—by utilizing a specific set of ingredients and putting those ingredients together in a specific sequence, you could overcome the unseen barrier and achieve "explosive" continuous improvement.

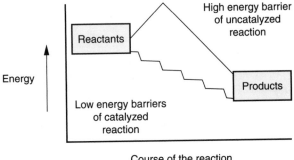

Figure 1.3   The catalyzed reaction.

OVERVIEW OF THE SIX KEY INGREDIENTS

So what are the catalysts or ingredients that enable the reaction to proceed successfully and the recipe for their implementation? After many years of directing continuous improvement programs in global companies, I have observed what has worked and what has not. All successful programs have the following ingredients:

1. Leadership commitment to drive the needed change

2. A clear strategic direction for the business or unit

3. An organized implementation plan designed to involve everybody

4. Training in the essential tools of improvement

5. A managed process to keep teams focused on projects critical to the success of the business

6. Meaningful rewards that maintain the momentum of the process

An organization's corporate culture sums up the character of that organization. The corporate culture reflects the values and philosophies of an enterprise, what is acceptable and unacceptable behavior within the organization, the managerial style that is perceived as most desirable, and the way work gets done. It reflects what is and what is not considered important by the organization. Although the culture builds over time, the most influential people are those at the top of the organization. They set the rules for others, and their behavior is the example that is followed. Top management is the only group that can ensure that continuous business improvement becomes a daily occurrence in the organization. Not only must the senior leaders commit to making it part of the culture, they must get involved and set the example for others throughout the business. Leadership commitment from the top is essential to develop a truly successful companywide program.

These same senior leaders also have the responsibility to develop the strategic direction for the business. They must decide which customers and markets the organization will serve and the manner in which the enterprise will compete. After setting the strategy, they must then communicate it effectively throughout the organization so that the whole workforce understands and commits to align its work in support. In world-class companies, there is excellent alignment and continuous effort to ensure that the work being done is adding value for customers and the bottom line.

In order that the improvement process itself does not create waste, it is necessary for the process to be well thought out and systematically introduced. I have seen many programs in which extensive training was completed in early stages but not used by the recipients, who then needed retraining by the time they actually began to work on teams. I have also seen teams working on projects that were meaningless to their organizations and had zero impact to the business once completed because there was no method in place to ensure people were working on the appropriate tasks.

The Recipe lays out a simple, effective path that any organization can follow. It is designed for small companies that do not have the capability to take on resource-intensive programs, such as Six Sigma. However, the Recipe will also work for large organizations in which the final solution is not yet decided because the Recipe starts the improvement process by providing all of the basic techniques needed to support any of the advanced methodologies, which can be added at a later time.

Education and training is necessary for people to understand why the organization has to embrace business improvement. Everyone in the organization must understand what the company has to do to survive the intense competitive environment in today's economy. Training is also essential to develop the high-performance teaming skills and investigative tools needed to find breakthrough methods of working. The most effective training not only teaches people new skills but also enables them to practice and use those tools immediately once trained. The training starts simple and then continues by adding new skills over time. It concentrates on making both individuals and teams more efficient and more effective in their work.

World-class business improvement processes have mechanisms in place to ensure that the right work is being done. World-class organizations tie improvement projects to the strategic direction of the business and to needed improvements, such as enhancing customer satisfaction or improving profitability. These organizations also have tight project management guidelines so that teams can operate efficiently and implement effective permanent solutions to problems.

Finally, world-class organizations have compensation, reward, and recognition programs that align the workforce, top to bottom, with their strategic direction and the business improvement process, which are designed to raise both the individual and collective performance to sustain the organizations' competitive capability.

ENDNOTE

1. John Hicks, *Comprehensive Chemistry,* 2nd ed. (New York: Macmillan Press, 1970).

2
Ingredient 1: Leadership Commitment

KEY ROLES OF LEADERS

In his book *Leadership Secrets of Attila the Hun,* Wess Roberts said, "Leadership is the privilege to have the responsibility to direct the actions of others in carrying out the purposes of the organization, at various levels of authority and with accountability for both successful and failed endeavors."[1] Leaders exist at all levels of an organization, but nowhere is leadership more important than at the top. The leader or group of leaders at the top has the awesome task of setting the future direction of the organization and the ultimate accountability for its prosperity or demise. Much has been written on the subject of what makes a good or bad leader, and it is not my intention to discuss that subject. Instead, I am going to discuss what roles leaders have to fulfill.

People who hold a leadership position at any level of a company have two functions they must do well: they must both lead and manage. The delineation between these two roles is often blurred, but both roles must be filled if the organization is to be successful.

Let's look at what comprises each function. The functions of leadership are:

- *Establishing strategic direction*—setting the vision and mission that will guide the organization

- *Aligning the people*—communicating the strategic direction and gaining commitment from everyone

- *Motivating and inspiring*—initiating and maintaining momentum to move the organization forward and overcome barriers

- *Producing change*—initiating change to make the organization better

The functions of management are:

- *Planning and budgeting*—setting the goals, targets, and timetable for the organization

- *Organizing and staffing*—developing the organization structure, positions, and roles to meet the budget

- *Controlling and problem solving*—monitoring compliance to the plan and intervening when needed to keep the plan on track

- *Maintaining predictability*—keeping the ship as steady as possible and preventing change in those areas in which it is not beneficial

Newly promoted managers in lower levels of an organization usually find that the majority of their work is biased toward the lower-level tasks of the management function. The strategic direction is set, their goals and targets are defined, and they have little authority to amend the staffing structure. They are expected to monitor, control, and keep their departments or units on track. In an enlightened organization, they might be expected to fulfill these roles using a coaching, involving, and persuading manner in order to inspire involvement from their staffs. However, more often than not, they are just expected to get the job done, no matter what it takes.

As these managers climb the ladder of success, the number of tasks they are expected to fulfill slowly increases until soon they are setting goals and deciding staffing levels for their departments or units. Only at the very top does the role of setting strategic direction and the ultimate goals of the organization occur. All lower levels are expected to follow the direction set at the top and align their department or unit goals with the corporate goals.

One reason why many managers struggle at the higher levels of organizations is that, having worked their way up through the ranks, they are well versed, practiced, and conditioned to the function of management but have little experience in the practice of leadership. There is also a major difference between playing and composing the tune. Many people can learn to play an instrument, but few musicians become great composers. In the business world, there are many managers who progress from being good managers to good leaders but few leaders become great strategists. Only great strategists can successfully steer their businesses through turbulent times.

However, the team at the top has no choice—the role of deciding where the business is going and how it will get there rests squarely on the leaders' shoulders. They have to decide what industry the enterprise will be involved in, what products or services will be produced, and which customers will be served and how. After they make these strategic decisions, they must continuously review how the organization is implementing the strategy in order to be a winning business. Often there are many competitors in a given industry and usually more than one of these competitors has an approach that can be considered successful. Like runners in a 1500-meter race, any competitor could win on any particular day, but in business there is no finish line.

Becoming world-class and remaining there takes a lot of hard work and continuous performance improvement. Consider the world of sport. Many of the great athletes who won gold medals in early Olympics would not even qualify today. Special diets, rigorous strength and conditioning training, and better equipment, clothing, and facilities have all contributed to incremental performance improvements. New techniques have also been developed that have resulted in step changes in performance. Take, for example, the high jump. Prior to the mid 1960s, there were two methods of getting over the bar: the western roll and the scissors. These methods are not even seen today, as everyone jumps with the *Fosbury flop*, a technique developed by Dick Fosbury prior to winning Olympic gold in 1968.

The same holds true for companies. Companies that use the training methodologies, techniques, equipment, and facilities of the past will no longer be able to compete effectively in today's business arena. Companies must continually improve to stay in the world-class pack. Therefore, producing change to make the organization better is a key leadership role.

In world-class organizations, the commitment to producing change is clearly understood and taken on by the highest-level leaders. They understand that the business improvement process must start with them. They realize that both their individual behavior and their collective performance as a team set the tone and standard for everyone else in the organization. They know that only they make or break the rules that the organization abides by. They know that if they want to banish bureaucracy and nurture a creative environment, they must make the first changes.

I have seen business improvement programs that have been started at lower levels of organizations by enthusiastic business unit leaders or function managers. However, most of those programs soon faded away. The only programs that were successful were those that were adopted by the leadership team and transformed into companywide programs. Leadership commitment is the number one ingredient for any successful business improvement process.

INSTIGATING THE REMOVAL OF WASTE TO FREE UP TIME FOR IMPROVEMENT

A powerful tool that leaders and managers at all levels can use to demonstrate their commitment and involvement in business improvement is the STOP process.

Start with yourself and ask the following questions:

1. What are your roles and responsibilities? Include your:

   - Job functions

   - Major goals

   - Key tasks

2. How do you accomplish these? Include the:

   - Tasks you do

   - Tasks you delegate

   - Meetings you attend

   - Reports you write and receive

3. What can you change? Include any task you can:

   - Eliminate

   - Combine

   - Simplify

The idea is to eliminate non-value-added tasks from your life forever. Do not put them on a *to do* list for later. STOP doing them.

When I first started using the STOP process, I found myself arguing the need to do things the same old way. After repeating this exercise on a regular basis, which ensured I kept focused on important tasks, I realized there were many areas where my efforts were wasteful. I found that 90 percent of the reports I sent out were not even read. I discovered that my deliberate absence from some meetings actually enhanced the decision-making capability of those who reported to me, and my own effectiveness and efficiency improved 100 percent or more—suddenly I had time to think.

A good example of what I later found to be a wasteful task was the monthly report I prepared while working as the head of quality in a major chemical company. I began to notice questions being asked of me in the management staff meetings that indicated people either had not received or had not read my monthly report. I checked to make sure they were receiving it, and they were. In the next report, about half way down the fifth page, I put the following sentence: "Congratulations on reading so far in this report—you may have won $10. Call Dave Till at 555-5555 and he'll be happy to pay the first caller."

I sent out the report as usual and waited, telling myself that, in the future, I would send the report only to the people who called. After three months of not sending the report to anyone, I got a call from my boss's secretary, who asked where my monthly reports were. When questioned how she had noticed, she replied there was a hole appearing in the file cabinet where she kept them!

There were also reports that I was receiving that I did not find useful, so I had a stamp made up that said, "I did not use this report—why was it sent to me?" I made a point of calling anyone who sent me such a report so that the person understood why I was asking the question. I also tried to coach the person, telling him or her to make sure the report was available to those people who did indeed need it but not to send it to anyone else because that is wasteful.

Once you are happy that you have completed the STOP process for yourself, take it to your team. By telling the team members how you have personally started to change, you set the example for them to follow. Repeat the exercise with your team. Ask each individual to go through the questions and share their answers with the rest of the team. Expose your own answers for feedback from the team. Don't be surprised if the team members have a different perspective than you about what you are or should be doing.

Managers often think their involvement in tasks is absolutely necessary and value-adding, while their staff members would be happier if the managers got out of the way so that they could do the work they were hired to do. Keep asking the questions: How does this add value? How does this fit with the vision, mission, and goals that are set? These questions might be uncomfortable for your team members, so be sensitive to that. Make the process easy for them. Help them realize that you are simply trying to help everyone become more effective by eliminating wasteful tasks and events, but be persistent.

In a manufacturing plant, the general manager was convinced that he needed to attend every coordination meeting that his production and engineering staff held. He told me his experience was that if he wasn't there to referee the discussions, the two groups could not come to an agreement. In order to attend every meeting, he was working 12-hour days. I observed several of these meetings and saw a different picture. As issues came up, the general manager would often jump in prematurely and make a decision based on his past experience, without letting the team members review the facts and come to their own conclusion.

When we held the STOP process session, the team members told him that they felt he was too controlling and by making all the decisions, he was not helping them to develop as individuals or a team. He reluctantly agreed to withdraw from some of the sessions, but as the team blossomed and posted facts and actions in the coordination war room that he could observe, he rapidly pulled out of all the sessions.

He had always been the last manager to turn in his budgets and plans, but now with more time to work on them, he performed better in that area and found he did not need to work 12-hour days any longer. He became more effective and efficient, and so did his team.

Once you have each individual feeling happy about what he or she is going to stop doing, address the work of the team. Identify the roles and responsibilities of the team as a whole. This is particularly important at the leadership level because there are issues that the team collectively must take care of—issues that transcend the functions of each individual. There might also be items that need to be accomplished that are not in any one specific job function but rather implicit in everyone's job, such as ensuring legal or fiduciary compliance. By identifying these items as a team responsibility, you can ensure they are maintained on the list of priorities.

Without this type of STOP process and priority review, many leadership teams become bogged down in the day-to-day problems that occur in any business. They become distracted from the important work that only the leaders can do. With the speed of change accelerating as it is today, companies that review and address strategies only once a year will not be able to compete with those companies that continuously devote time to strategic thinking and to building flexibility and rapid response into their organizations. The only way that leaders can find the time for these activities is to stop doing the unimportant tasks.

The same rule also applies for a team that is brought together for a business improvement project. Most employees are fully occupied in the jobs they perform. In many project situations, no consideration is given to how the selected employees will find the time to participate. An assumption is made that they will somehow find the time for the added responsibilities.

Teams that are chartered in this way will struggle to perform, and some of the individuals will become extremely stressed as they try to cope with the extra burden. Your company cannot afford to follow this practice. The projects described in this book are important to your business. You want the projects to be successful, so you must afford the team members every chance to be successful. To do so, you need to use the STOP process each time a team is started. Make it a rule that the team's sponsor and the supervisors of the team members must attend the kick-off meeting and help the team eliminate some non-value-added tasks. As much as 50 percent of employees' time might be spent on non-value-added tasks. By eliminating these tasks, you'll free up the time the employees need to be successful. By initiating the STOP process, you will also be raising the performance of the whole organization because wasteful tasks will be eliminated each time a project is started.

ACTIVELY LEADING CONTINUOUS BUSINESS IMPROVEMENT

In the early 1990s, I was based in a corporate headquarters in a large American city. The company occupied two floors, and the executive offices were located at the southern end of the lower floor. The chief executive officer (CEO), all of the vice presidents (VPs), and all their assistants were in this area, which was cordoned off from the rest of the workforce. At both entrances into the executive area were glass doors with electronic locks. Only those people with key access could enter. Anyone who was called to a meeting had to be buzzed in by one of the assistants.

In 1997, the CEO was succeeded by an outsider who was determined to change the culture of the business from exclusion to involvement. He was officially appointed on a Friday and his first action was the removal of the doors. He felt this was such an important message to send to the workforce that he had the doors removed on Saturday so the people would be greeted on Monday with the new open environment.

Imagine his surprise when, by Wednesday, not one person had ventured into the area from which the employees had previously been barred. Only after he began to tour the general area every day, inviting people back to the executive area, did the invisible barrier begin to disintegrate and the spirit of openness begin to grow. Even after some months there were still some skeptics who were convinced the change was only temporary and spent many of their working hours looking for the evidence to prove it so.

Next, the CEO began to have the VPs move their offices into the general area. I was the first department head to move my office into the midst of the people who worked for me. When the company relocated to a new building a few years later, there was no executive area—all the VPs were out in their work groups. The cultural change had taken hold.

The invisible barrier exists in every change situation! A successful change cannot be accomplished by wishing it so. There have to be behavioral modifications. In the business world, employees watch how managers at every level act and follow the examples they *see* rather than taking guidance from the words they *hear*. If you want employees to behave differently, then as a senior manager, you have to teach and show them how you want them to act. Unless you *show* them, most people will be frozen in the old culture unable to move, even if you've told them about the change.

In the business improvement arena, the most successful programs have senior leaders who take this challenge personally and become directly involved in the process of breaking both visible and invisible barriers and who actively coach and encourage individuals and teams to make the breakthroughs needed. To do this, these leaders need to understand the process, the basic tools, and what questions to ask. Then they need to actively demonstrate their understanding and commitment to the program.

All managers should be able to state with clarity the vision for the business and the missions of all departments. They should be able to state with passion the mission of their own department and what activities are going on under their control to meet their goals. Ensuring that this clarity exists throughout the business is the first role of senior managers. In meetings, senior managers need to challenge managers to explain what their departments are doing and how they ensure alignment with the vision and mission. Making sure the message is getting out and being understood at all levels is the second role of senior managers. They should question the folks on the shop floor. Have they received training on the business improvement methodology? Do they understand why, what, and how changes are being made? Do they understand how they can help?

The behavioral changes needed to develop a world-class business improvement approach do not come naturally to most people. Many people set New Year's resolutions they strongly desire to keep, but within a few weeks they are back in their old routine with no hope of real change. For example, many people promise to exercise but fail to make it part of their daily routine, so they do it only sporadically. Even those people who have a medical necessity to exercise find it extremely difficult to make the change, especially if they are comfortable in their present routine.

The way to overcome this natural tendency to resist change is to have a specific timetable for the new events that have to occur, which will make the change real and sustained. The timetable needs to have employees frequently repeat the behavior so that it becomes a habit. After it becomes a habit, the behavior will stay part of the employees' routine until you want to change the behavior again.

For all managers, the change starts with the STOP process. After you have completed this process for yourself and have decided which tasks you will stop working on, set aside 10 minutes each day to review how you are doing. Looking back over the previous 48 hours, have you stayed the course or have you strayed and done some tasks you promised to stop doing?

If things have not gone according to plan, you need to determine what caused you to go off track. However, don't make excuses if you spent time on unimportant or wasteful tasks. Recognize it and move on. Figure out what you're going to do that will enable you to stay focused. You will make sustainable change only if you work at it.

I like to start each day with this 10-minute review; it keeps me focused on that day's actions. I know other people like to end their day with reflection while setting their timetable. Whatever works for you is good.

While the team is going through the change process, set up a similar 10-minute review process for your team at the start of each weekly team meeting. If the team meets only monthly, hold a short teleconference each week to review progress during the first eight weeks of the STOP process.

Prompt your managers and their teams to follow a similar timetable. Review with each manager how that person and his or her teams are managing to follow the STOP process. A 10-minute session once a week should suffice.

Next comes project tracking. In the first week, set aside enough time to review all projects that are currently being worked on. Each project should be reviewed to check that it meets the following criteria:

1. Does the project fit with the strategy?

2. Will the project help to better meet customer needs?

3. Compared with external and internal benchmarks, is the performance trend poor so that there is plenty of room for improvement?

4. Will the project be easy to accomplish?

If a project does not meet all the criteria, you have a team that is working in an area that is unimportant to the business. You must disband this team, but you must do so with care! The team members need to know it is not their fault that the project is being terminated. Explain in detail to them that the project is being terminated because it does not meet the criteria.

When possible, try to reassign team members to a project that does meet the criteria. If this is impossible, continue their training and assign them to a project as soon as possible.

The whole workforce also needs to know why a project was terminated. You can provide this information through a newsletter or memo, then reinforce the message with verbal communications.

If during your review of the projects you find there are critical business issues not being addressed, add projects in those areas. The best way to do this would be for the leadership team to spend the day together reviewing and debating the value of each proposed project to determine which projects need to be added. Doing this as a team reinforces the alignment that needs to be created between the projects and the company's strategies.

After the list of new projects is complete, define who owns them. A senior leader should own all projects in his or her functional area and be responsible for tracking and reporting progress. After all the new projects have owners, ask each manager to review them and identify potential gains. These new projects should then be put on a 90-day cycle.

The new projects' progress should be reviewed at 30 days, 60 days, and 90 days, when hopefully they're completed. The senior leader does not need to attend all of the 30-, 60-, and 90-day reviews, but someone in authority does in order to emphasize the importance of the projects. The senior leaders must attend as many reviews as possible to place the needed emphasis on the business improvement process.

Table 2.1 shows the weekly time commitment leaders and managers must make in the first three months of the business improvement process.

During each quarter, senior managers are asked to devote a total of 48 hours, or six days, of direct involvement. In a 13-week period, there are 65 normal working days, so you are committing less than 10 percent of your time to a program that can double the bottom-line profit over two to three years.

Table 2.1 Weekly tasks.

Week	Task	Time
1	STOP process for yourself	4 hours
2	STOP process for team	1 day
3	Initial project review with team	1 day
4	30-day review	1 day
8	60-day review	1 day
12	90-day review	1 day
13	Celebration lunch	4 hours

Table 2.2 Daily tasks.

Day	Task	Time
Monday	STOP process for yourself STOP process for your team STOP process for your managers (two manager sessions per day)	10 minutes 10 minutes 20 minutes
Tuesday, Thursday, and Friday	STOP process for yourself STOP process for your managers	10 minutes 20 minutes
Wednesday	STOP process for yourself STOP process for your reports Projects review	10 minutes 20 minutes 30 minutes

Table 2.2 shows the ongoing weekly commitment needed to sustain the process.

You need to give three hours and 10 minutes of your week to sustain the process, which is less than 10 percent of the usual 40-hour week and less than 5 percent of the work week of most senior managers and executives. And, remember, the STOP process will be freeing up time—my experience is that by following this process, you will work fewer hours overall.

A MANUFACTURING COMPANY EXAMPLE

Let's look at my experience of working with the leadership team of a manufacturing company as an example. The team went through a weekend retreat and came up with the following roles that they had to accomplish as a team:

1. Strategic planners:

   • Establish vision, mission, and strategic objectives for the business.

   • Review and approve strategic plans for each department.

   • Provide resources and support to achieve strategic objectives.

2. Business process owners:

   • Continuously improve the processes required to run the enterprise.

   • Resolve process interface issues to optimize overall performance of the organization.

3. Managers of goals and objectives:

   • Develop and approve operating and capital budgets.

   • Ensure all departments and individuals are aligned with objectives.

   • Anticipate and proactively develop plans to overcome barriers

4. Leaders of culture change:

   • Establish high-performance operating style.

   • Ensure corporate values are demonstrated.

   • Set the example for expected team behavior.

   • Ensure the collective development of people across the organization.

5. Communicators:

   • Reinforce the company's values and beliefs in both actions and words.

   • Ensure that the vision, mission, strategies, and objectives are understood throughout the organization.

   • Provide periodic updates to all employees on business performance and issues.

   • Be ambassadors to the outside world.

In going through this team review, the leaders realized that they were spending too much of their time working at issues that belonged lower in the organization. They were not paying enough attention to the changing nature of the business. The existing strategic review was a paperwork exercise that had resulted in a doorstop-sized book to which no one ever referred. The business was changing rapidly: customers were now shopping in the global marketplace, and new competitors from Asia were attacking strongly with me-too products. The team began to meet more frequently to improve the company's competitive response, and it did so with renewed vigor.

The leaders were leaving business process change to the quality group, which was struggling with the bureaucracy present in many areas. The leaders accepted responsibility at the lead team level and cut through the red tape, which gave a new energy to the program.

By coming together as a team to own all the goals of the business, the leaders were able to provide the time that the groups needed to meet critical priorities. For example, the leaders worked with the manufacturing group to free up the time that the R&D group needed to experiment with new products. Previously, this time was not made available because the manufacturing group charged after their department goals of maximizing output. The leaders also set aside time to coach and develop the next level of potential leaders. Leadership development previously was handled within departments. Although the departments had many functional experts, no one was available to develop the general managers and strategists needed for the future.

Scoreboards were established in each area of the business and updated monthly, which kept all employees informed about the progress toward the mission. Meetings were held regularly to discuss progress and listen to how people thought the progress could be accelerated. Within a short time, everyone in the organization knew the vision for the future, the current mission, the goals to achieve, and the tasks that were important and needing attention.

The leadership team was clearly spearheading the push for business improvement in order to meet the strategic needs of the company. And a freshly inspired workforce was eagerly following.

ENDNOTE

1. Wess Roberts, *Leadership Secrets of Attila the Hun* (New York: Warner Books, 1987).

3

Ingredient 2: Strategic Alignment

KNOWING WHERE THE BUSINESS IS GOING

Figure 3.1 shows a model that depicts a business as a system of internal processes competing with other businesses in the same industry for the same external resources and the same customers. When many managers view their business in this way, they believe that the way to compete is to make their internal processes better than those of their competitors. For this reason, many continuous improvement initiatives focus on cost reduction and a belief that, by serving customers better (having a customer focus), they will gain market share and become more profitable.

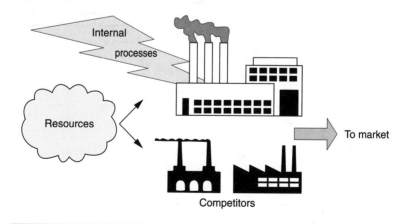

Figure 3.1   Simple business model.

According to Chris Zook and James Allen in their book *Profit from the Core*, the Bain consulting group maintains a database that shows that the best-performing companies in a particular industry or segment (the companies with the best returns for shareholders) are those that lead the rate of growth within that segment. Typically, these companies grow at two to three times the average for their industry segment.[1] Further, their growth is often driven by their leadership position in one or two core businesses, with expansion occurring into adjacent businesses in which their core capabilities can be exploited. Look at General Electric (GE) as an example. Table 3.1 shows GE's revenue and earnings growth for the past 11 years.

GE has five core businesses and four key areas that drive business growth. According to GE's Web site, the four areas are:

- *Globalization*—finding the best resources from all over the world
- *Services*—improving the installed base through reengineering
- *Digitization*—aggressive use of technology
- *Six Sigma*—elimination of all defects

Motorola's growth has also been impressive, as Table 3.2 shows. Motorola describes the events that contributed to its growth in its Web site's history section, which is devoted to impressing potential investors. Motorola states that Six Sigma was implemented during the mid 1980s.

Table 3.1 GE's growth.

Year	Revenue ($ Billion)	Operating Income ($ Billion)
1992	53	4.1
1993	56	4.2
1994	66	5.9
1995	70	6.5
1996	79	7.3
1997	91	8.2
1998	100	9.3
1999	112	10.7
2000	130	12.7
2001	126	14.1
2002	132	15.1

Source: GE annual reports

Table 3.2 Motorola's growth.

Year	Revenue ($ billion)	Net Profit ($ billion)
1980	3.1	0.2
1990	11	0.5
2000	36.5	1.8

Source: Motorola Web site

You can clearly see that both Motorola and GE had major growth strategies. Both companies implemented Six Sigma programs to support those strategies.

Given that the best performers are growing at a pace faster than their competitors, companies need to focus on how to successfully implement then continually improve the growth process. This is fundamentally the role of senior management in any company. Senior managers should be spending the majority of their time and effort developing the strategies of how to beat their competition in the growth race.

When senior managers look at the business model in Figure 3.1, they should be picturing themselves as working *on* the system rather than *in* the system in the effort to improve overall performance. Their role is to decide how the organization will go to market and what products, services, and channels will be used. The questions they need to answer include:

- What key processes should exist in the organization in order to support the quest to win in the marketplace?

- How should the organization be structured and staffed to enable successful execution of those processes?

- Which suppliers can actively support the growth and become partners with the organization?

Further, senior managers need to assess what the competitors are currently doing and how they can be expected to behave in the future. Senior managers must do this strategic work—no one else in the organization can be expected to do it.

The traditional model for describing strategic choices is shown in Figure 3.2. I first came across this model in my strategic management studies for my Master's degree in business administration (MBA).[2] There are four quadrants in which growth can be accomplished. Quadrant one is the current marketplace in which your company supplies its existing products and services to existing customers. Growth is enabled by making

Products and services	*New*	Product development *Quadrant 3*	Diversification *Quadrant 4*
	Present	Market penetration *Quadrant 1*	Market development *Quadrant 2*
		Present	*New*
		Markets	

Figure 3.2   Traditional strategic model.

improvements or reducing costs so that customers are prepared to make a larger portion of their purchases with your company, at the expense of current competitors, because your company is a better supplier. Unless handled carefully, this strategy can rapidly become a defensive posture; in order to survive, all improvements are directed toward reducing costs just to stay in business. In quadrant two, existing products are introduced to new markets typically through geographic expansion. In quadrant three, new products are introduced to the existing market, usually through research and development (R&D) activities. Quadrant four involves moving to related markets in which the core competencies can be exploited or taking ventures into unknown territory, which might be risky. History shows that such ventures have been the downfall of many companies.

From a continuous improvement perspective, it is better to view the strategic model as Figure 3.3 shows. In this model, there is a sort of natural progression through the strategic choices, from easiest to most difficult to implement. For a company to grow to where it wants to be in the future, it is essential to improve performance in its existing business. The existing business has to generate the financial returns needed to enable investments in future growth ventures. Without a successful track record in the existing business, senior managers will be unable to convince shareholders to invest in what they will inevitably see as more risky propositions.

This book is not about strategic management. The point I'm trying to make is that any business improvement program must be aligned with the strategic direction of the business—and the role of accomplishing that

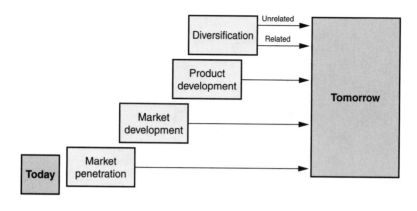

Figure 3.3   Strategic progression model.

alignment rests squarely on the shoulders of the senior leaders. It is not a role that can be delegated to some business improvement champion or team. Implicit in that role is the fact that senior leaders must know and approve every project to ensure it's in alignment.

If you are a senior manager wrestling with the responsibility of deriving the strategy for your business, I recommend you read *The Power of Strategic Thinking* by Michel Robert,[3] *Profit from the Core,*[4] and *The New Corporate Strategy* by H. Igor Ansoff.[5] These three books will broaden anyone's insights into strategic management and help you come up with that winning strategy.

THE CASCADING PROCESS FOR SETTING GOALS THROUGHOUT THE ORGANIZATION

After the strategy is set, the next step is to use a cascading process to develop missions for each function and the goals and milestones that will enable project activity and performance monitoring to start. Figure 3.4 gives an overview of the cascading process for setting goals and choosing projects. This process starts with the strategic vision for the business, then flows down through the mission and goals for each department, and finally cascades down to two or three important projects for each department to work on. The key to this process is to maintain focus and keep the number of goals

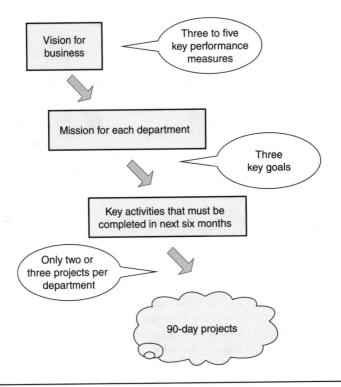

Figure 3.4   The cascading process.

down to three to five for each department. Set only those goals that are critical to the success of the business. Many companies get carried away and have a whole slew of goals for each department and 10 or so goals for individuals. Having too many goals blurs the focus on the key items that must be accomplished and dilutes the improvement effort across too broad an array of actions. Having too many goals also induces the start-up of too many projects. Managers often feel the need to have action going on in all of the areas in which they have goals. So, if they have 10 goals, they are likely to start 10 projects. Wanting to ensure success, some managers even start two projects for each goal and have 20 projects running.

In my earlier years of running business improvement projects, I was guilty of making this mistake. I discovered that when the process involved too many projects, there was a proportionately increased level of failed projects because the resources were not there to support them. I used to say if you start 90 projects, 30 would never seriously get off the ground, 30 would be incomplete by the end of the year, and 30 would deliver. I now believe that by focusing on fewer goals, critical issues, and only those projects that count, each team can deliver success. In addition, the teams' results will have a much greater impact on the fortunes of the business.

SETTING THE CRITERIA THAT ENSURE PROJECTS ARE CONTRIBUTING TO THE BUSINESS IMPROVEMENT PROCESS

Figure 3.5 shows an overview of the criteria (in descending order) that should be used to identify and prioritize projects. When selecting projects, you need to answer four questions:

1. *Does the project fit with the company's strategy?* I once came across a business in which the owners were extremely worried that more than 70 percent of their products were sold to just one customer. Thus, the company's strategy was to reduce its dependence on this one outlet by developing new products in order to expand the client base. However, the

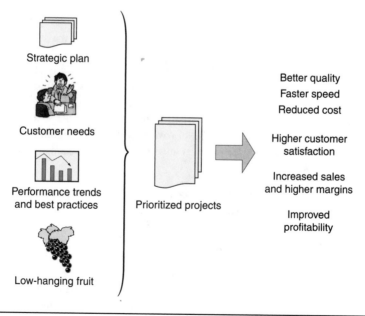

Figure 3.5 Criteria for project selection.

company had almost all of its R&D resources tied into joint projects with the major customer to enhance existing products. Even though it was a delicate task, the company reduced its involvement in order to work on new developments. The owners have now expanded their business significantly. The company still has its one major customer, but now it has only 30 percent of its revenues tied to that one client. No company can afford to tie up resources on projects that do not match the strategic direction of the business.

2. *Will the project help to better meet customers' needs?* Even in the case just noted, the joint projects being run were not necessarily in the best interests of the customer. By spending time enhancing old products, the company was not keeping its customer abreast of the latest technologies available that could improve the customer's competitiveness. By switching resources to develop new products, the company was able to help its major customer improve its offering in the marketplace. Projects that help your customers' competitive position are always good because they increase your potential business. Also, projects that correct deficiencies that customers perceive in your products or services will help you stay in business.

3. *Compared with external and internal benchmarks, is the performance trend poor so there is plenty of room for improvement?* Suppose that a plant has two manufacturing lines that essentially produce the same product. The first line makes 10 percent scrap, whereas the second line has less than two percent scrap. There should be ample opportunity to get the scrap down on the first line because better performance is already being demonstrated elsewhere. If the industry standard for these products is a two percent scrap rate, it would be extremely difficult to improve the second line, which is already operating at the best proven level. At the beginning of the improvement process, choose projects in which there is a reasonable chance of success.

4. *Will the project be easy to accomplish?* When I was living in the beautiful Wye valley in Chepstow, Wales, there were a number of proposals to build a second crossing over the Severn river, which separated England and Wales. The traffic flow was too heavy for the existing bridge. One of the proposals was to build a dam across the estuary that would contain enough turbines to generate one-sixth of Britain's requirements for electricity. Traffic would pass along the top of the dam. Although the project was feasible, it was totally impractical because of the time it would take to build the dam. So, a second bridge was chosen as the reasonable

solution. Choose projects that will likely have practical solutions. It is especially beneficial to choose those projects that have many potential paths for team members to explore.

Taking the time to choose the best projects pays off in the long run. If projects are chosen well, the outcomes should provide better quality, faster speed, and reduced costs, which leads to higher customer satisfaction, increased sales, and higher profitability.

COMMUNICATING TO EMPLOYEES SO THAT THEY UNDERSTAND AND HELP

After the strategy has been set and the links to cascading goals and key projects have been established, the final step is to communicate the program throughout the company. Who are the key people in your organization who need to know about the program? Everybody.

By knowing the vision, mission, goals, and key projects, everyone in the business can gauge whether the work he or she is doing is contributing.

How often should people be communicated to? Continuously. The best companies use visual aids at every opportunity. Your business should do the same by posting the company's vision, mission, and goals everywhere. Start by having the CEO or president and some of his or her reports make a videotape outlining the vision, mission, and what the company is doing to move forward. This videotape can be created with a simple home video camera. The credibility of the message is what's important, not the professionalism of the videotape. Send multiple copies around the company so that the videotape can be shown to the workforce as part of the kickoff meetings. Make individual departments post their goals and projects, and have every VP, director, manager, and supervisor discuss how the company is doing relative to the overall goals at every opportunity.

At least monthly, send updates through the ranks and have informal discussions about those updates. If you have a company newsletter, you can include the updates in it. Better still, you can generate a monthly newsletter devoted solely to the program. Like the videotape, the monthly newsletter does not need to be fancy. You can simply produce the document in a word-processing program such as Microsoft Word. What's important is that the newsletter keeps on reinforcing the message of the vision, mission, and how the projects tie in. You can even have teams contribute summaries of the projects they are working on.

Check the communication frequently. Is the message getting through? All of the employees will appreciate open, honest communication that keeps them abreast of where the company is headed, how the business is performing, and how they can help. The major purposes of communication are to maintain alignment and to encourage involvement. The best companies use both formal and informal communication to ensure their workforce is kept as well informed as possible.

A CHEMICAL COMPANY EXAMPLE

To illustrate the importance of strategic alignment, let me use an example of a chemical company that was international in scope, with manufacturing concentrated in North America and Europe. This company's vision was to become the global leader (or a strong number two) in its industry. Table 3.3 shows the company's key measures and goals.

In defining these key measures and goals, the company recognized several issues:

- Growth could be accomplished only if the existing business generated better returns.

- Either new plants or acquisitioned plants would be needed in both Latin America and Asia.

- The company was not structured to support acquisitions. Although it had an engineering department that could design and build new facilities, none of the people had any experience with acquisitions or with operating in Latin America or Asia.

The president set up a new acquisitions division in the company to handle these issues. The VP who headed this new division was charged with bringing into the organization people who had the acquisitions and geographic expertise needed. (Remember, only the senior leader and his or her team can change the structure of the organization.) Here is how the

Table 3.3   The chemical company's key measures and goals.

Key Measures	Current	Target
Sales Revenue	$300 million	$900 million
Market Share • North America • Europe • Latin America • Asia	15% 15% 0% 0%	25% 25% 15% 15%
Profitability	$50 million	$200 million

company rolled its vision into the mission and the goals of the sales and manufacturing departments.

For the Sales Group

Mission: transition from a regional to a global sales system that can grow sales in existing markets and capture higher market share in new geographical areas.

Three Key Goals

1. Increase market share in North America and Europe from 15 percent to 25 percent while improving profitability.

2. Establish export process to penetrate chosen expansion markets to establish brand name and ready market to support manufacturing facility in the region.

3. Establish sales offices in Asia and Latin America.

Project Teams

1. Existing market growth: improve sales and profitability by leveraging technology in product range. Team members are from sales, R&D, and manufacturing.

2. Export: establish process for low-cost distribution of current products to Latin America and Asia. Team members are from sales, the supply group, and the new acquisitions division.

3. Sales office: determine office locations in Asia and Latin America. Team members are senior sales leaders.

For the Manufacturing Group

Mission: Increase output in North America and Europe to meet sales growth needs with minimum capital expenditure. (Capital needed for Latin America and Asia projects.)

Three Key Goals

1. Increase throughput by 20 percent in existing operations.

2. Reduce number of customer issues to enable capture of greater market share.

3. Reduce cost of operations by 5 percent to improve profitability.

Project Teams

1. Bottleneck removal: define constraints at each manufacturing plant and determine best practice to remove them. Team members are from manufacturing, engineering, and R&D.

2. Yield improvement: improve chemical yields through optimization. Team members are from manufacturing, purchasing, and R&D.

The Results

As the manufacturing teams worked, they quickly found that, contrary to popular belief, small components in the plants were the major constraints. Items such as fans and pumps were causing problems rather than the major capital items. Soon, and for very little expenditure, plants had 15 percent to 20 percent higher output levels.

By using different raw materials for different products, the manufacturing group also increased the chemical yield on many lines by 5 percent.

The sales group learned how to listen better to its customers. It modified several products and soon was winning market share at higher profitability levels.

The export levels grew and the company's brand name became better known in the target expansion regions. Competitors in those regions started to court the company as potential partners, trying to learn how to produce their products at the higher quality and performance levels.

The acquisitions division soon targeted Brazil and Taiwan as new areas for geographic expansion. They were able to "sell" the improvements made by manufacturing and license partnerships in those regions. The licensee partners, in turn, became joint ventures and subsidiaries. After only three years, the company was clearly number two in the industry and growing faster than any of its competitors.

This example describes only the process as it was applied to the sales and manufacturing groups. The system also was used across the whole business. For example, the HR function improved the hiring process to support the growth, the financial processes were changed to give time for better financial analysis, and the IT group made sure systems could be easily integrated. Total alignment occurred.

ENDNOTES

1. Chris Zook with James Allen, *Profit from the Core: Growth Strategy in an Era of Turbulence* (Boston: Harvard Business School Press, 2001).
2. Figure 3.2 is the brainchild of H. I. Ansoff. He later extended this matrix in H. Igor Ansoff, *The New Corporate Strategy* (New York: John Wiley & Sons, 1988).
3. Michel Robert, *The Power of Strategic Thinking: Lock in Markets, Lock out Competitors* (New York: McGraw-Hill Trade, 1999).
4. Zook with Allen.
5. Ansoff.

4

Ingredient 3: Organized Plan of Action

STUMBLING TO THE SOLUTION

In the early years of my involvement with business improvement, much of the process was trial and error. When I was first appointed to a position responsible for corporate-wide quality and continuous improvement, I was told "just go do it." I had no idea where to start, so I began to look at what other companies were doing. Every time I passed through an airport I would browse the bookstore and pick up the latest management book that I felt was relevant.

One such book was *In Search of Excellence* by Thomas J. Peters and Robert H. Waterman. They studied 62 companies to determine what made an excellent company.[1] In a follow-up report on quality that was based on the data from the initial research, Peters revealed what he called the six attributes of successful quality improvement programs[2]:

- Top management time and persistence

- Clear system (a consistently applied, structured system that includes measurement and training components)

- Constant stimulation

- Not limited to operations or manufacturing

- People centered, not machine based

- The drive for quality improvement includes achieving simplicity of design or procedure, which yields cost reductions

I also picked up pointers from seminars, colleagues, events, and other sources. For example, I visited the headquarters of Milliken & Company in Spartanburg, South Carolina, to attend a seminar. From that experience I learned how a company can change its system from the scientific management approach to a total customer-responsive model.

A fellow student in my MBA course enlightened me on the progress being made at HP's plant in Bristol, England. From him I learned about how to improve quality, productivity, and flexibility with a management approach that incorporates customer focus, management commitment, total participation, and systematic analysis.

I attended a Xerox quality day in Rochester, New York, as a supplier representative. From David Kearns, who was the CEO at the time, I learned about that company's quality program. He said it was "a massive long-term effort to embed quality into every crevice of our organization and to make continuous quality improvement a way of life." He went on to discuss the implementation strategy, which had five elements:

- Total commitment of senior management

- Quantifiable standards and measurements

- Education and training

- Recognitions and rewards

- Effective and consistent communication

Finally, I reviewed the quality programs in many other companies, such as Tennant's Quest for Quality program, Union Carbide's EQ program, and the quality programs in those Japanese companies that now had manufacturing facilities in Europe and the United States. In almost every case, I found evidence of leadership from the top, strong education and training programs, performance measures (including benchmarking against competitors and best performers), and recognition and reward programs to stimulate the change program and encourage employee involvement. Further, the Japanese companies' successful U.S. and European operations demonstrated that national culture was not important. American and European workers performed equally well as Japanese workers, which was good to know since I was about to implement a quality process in a company with four plants in the United States and one plant each in Germany, Italy, Spain, and England.

Based on all that I learned, I put a plan together. To show management commitment, I decided to bring together all of the senior managers for a three-day seminar. They would receive the education and training they needed to lead the process. The company would then launch an extensive training program using outside experts to teach teamwork and the statistical tools needed. Each senior manager would be responsible for all projects within his or her functional area. The target would be to have 100 projects under way within the first year. Based on their performance, teams would be rewarded with hats, T-shirts, and jackets bearing the company logo.

A year quickly passed by. Of the 10 senior managers, only one had truly bought into the process and was actively tracking his projects, eight had handed the job down to one of their direct reports, and one was actively campaigning to have the whole process stopped because it was diverting attention from what he believed were the real needs of the business. Of the 100 projects started, only 30 had resulted in a true measurable gain for the business. Although many employees attended training classes, some of them either refused to participate on teams or did not exhibit the skills they were trained in while they were on a team. The company had spent around $1 million on the training programs, so the overall process was break-even at best.

I survived another year by pointing out to my boss that the gurus said the process took time to implement and by promising significant results from the second year of the program. The program was then modified with the following changes:

- My boss was asked to "command and control" the participation of his direct reports (a task which I must say he relished).

- The senior managers were held responsible for ensuring that the projects related directly to the strategy of the business, were quantifiable, and produced results (20 percent of their bonus was tied to the achievement of results).

- Fewer projects were undertaken. Each project was determined by running a diagnostic on the business unit to quantify the opportunity for improvement.

- Teams were trained as they began the project, not before.

- Hats, T-shirts, and jackets were given out to recognize participation. Substantial nonmonetary gifts were given to successful teams.

- The senior managers met monthly to define issues, implement corrections to the program, and report on successes.

By the end of the second year, the projects had added almost $10 million to the bottom line. The program was deemed a success.

THE THREE SIMULTANEOUS PATHS TO RAPID BOTTOM-LINE IMPROVEMENT

Over the years, further modifications have been made to the process, which has evolved into the *concurrent approach* portrayed in Figure 4.1. As I described in chapter 3, the whole process starts with senior managers defining the strategic direction and key performance measures of the business. The business's performance measures cascade to the department level. Each department uses the performance measures to create its mission and key goals. At this point, the business improvement process kicks into action. The process's three-pronged approach is designed to occur concurrently. However, a little preparation before going into action will speed the process. Let's look at each of the prongs and how you can prepare for them.

EDUCATION FOR ALL

Education is needed to ensure everyone in the company understands:

- Why the program is being implemented

- What is involved in the implementation process and what each individual is expected to do to support the program

- How the implementation plan will proceed, how the projects and teams will be defined, and how the results will be measured

This education process should start at the top and cascade through every level of the organization. The presented material should be as clear and concise as possible and should be deliverable in a two- or three-hour session. Senior managers should give the presentation to middle managers who, in turn, should give it to their work groups, and so on. (Nothing makes you listen and learn better than the knowledge that you have to present the material.) At the main facilities, the senior managers should be present at the other sessions to answer questions and to show their commitment to the program. The presentation should include the following.

Why

In the "why" portion of the presentation, you need to describe the forces driving change: customers, competitors, and technology. You should show how customers are more demanding, want better value, are better informed and prepared, and have more choices than ever before. You should show how competitors can come from anywhere in the world, are better prepared

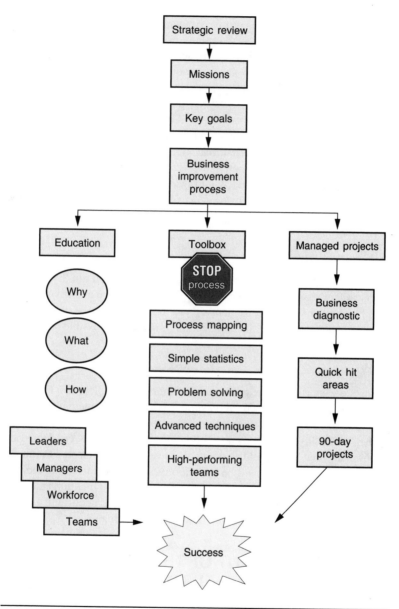

Figure 4.1   Concurrent business improvement methodology.

to fight for business, and can surprise you with new products, new processes, or new ways of doing business. You should show how technology is impacting your business, changing the marketplace, and making it hard to stay ahead.

You should include examples from your business, your customers, and your competitors. However, generic examples can also help. Aviation- or sports-related examples work well for illustrating how fast the world is changing and the importance of keeping abreast of those changes. A great example I like to use is the track and field record for the mile. In 1954, Roger Bannister became the first man to run a mile in less than 4 minutes, a feat that the medical profession in that era thought impossible. In the 1996 Olympics in Atlanta, Bannister would have been almost half a lap behind the group finishing the 1500-meter race. (The 1500-meter has replaced the mile as the world turns metric.)

What

In the "what" portion of the presentation, you need to roll out the strategic vision and targets for the business, along with the mission and key goals for each function and subunit. Remember you are trying to drive alignment of the organization, so make the explanation as simple as possible.

How

In the "how" portion of the presentation, you need to explain that there will be a number of projects focused on supporting the key strategy that will be put in place. You should note that these projects will be selected on the basis of their criticality to the business following the diagnostics conducted by senior managers. You should also note that teams will be selected to run the projects, and these teams will be trained on specific tools from the toolbox and managed to conclusion over 90 days. Don't forget to mention that, over time, almost everyone in the business will have the opportunity to be trained in these tools as project teams start up in each area.

DEVELOPMENT OF THE BEGINNER'S ESSENTIAL TOOLBOX

Let's now look at the toolbox and consider which tools should be in it.

Although the advanced techniques of Six Sigma and lean manufacturing have proven effective, many organizations do not have the resource base to be able to allocate full-time associates to the positions of Black Belts and lean masters, or go through the extensive training programs required to establish these programs. By following the Recipe and starting with just the essential tools, you will be able to make significant gains over the first year while you learn more about which of the advanced techniques could be incorporated into your program at a later time.

Just like a mechanic's toolbox or a carpenter's tool chest, the team member's toolbox should start with simple tools and build over time. The tools that are the easiest to use and that will be used most frequently are the STOP process, process mapping, the seven simple statistical tools, and simple problem solving. These tools, along with a little team training and facilitation, are sufficient to start a business improvement project that goes after the low-hanging fruit.

Just like apprentices, team members should master the basic tools before advancing to complex tools. These basic tools are the platform for all business improvement and are the starting point for all of the advanced techniques. Here is a quick overview of the toolbox tools. (I'll cover them in more depth in chapter 5.)

The STOP Process

The STOP process is a commonsense approach to finding the time for teams to work on problem solving. It is based on the statement: "In order to *start* doing something new you have to *stop* doing something old."

In many companies, stopping non-value-added work is very difficult. Employees might know that some of the reports they generate never get read, that some of the work they do is repeated by someone else, and that the invoices they send out will be returned by customers because the invoice software does not present the data the way the customers want it, but the employees are powerless to change the situation. Led by senior management, the STOP process can eliminate unnecessary work and reporting within weeks. It can free up the organization to work on important tasks.

Process Mapping

Process mapping is a tool that is used to help understand what is happening in a process. Essentially, it is a method to produce a diagram that depicts the activities occurring in a process.

The critical activities are identified first and put down in sequence on a large sheet of paper. The diagram should start out as simple as possible because everyone working on the project reviews and amends it. I like to have the team draw the diagram on flipchart-sized paper that can be pinned to the wall of the team room. That way, the diagram can be continuously reviewed and revised during the team's work periods. After the team agrees on the overall picture, the detail is slowly filled in as the team gathers data about what is happening within the process.

The Seven Simple Statistical Tools

The seven simple statistical tools (see page 58) are used to gather the data about the process:

- Flowchart
- Pareto chart
- Histogram
- Run chart
- Correlation chart
- Fishbone diagram
- Control chart

Simple Problem Solving

Once the process is well detailed and the facts are out on the table, the problem-solving stage is entered. For many problems, the clarity of understanding the issue through process mapping, data gathering, and presentation in the simple statistical charts leads to commonsense solutions.

One of the most widespread problem-solving approaches is to brainstorm potential solutions and then try the solutions. To solve complex issues, advanced techniques might be needed.

MANAGED TEAMS AND PROJECTS

Compared with other business improvement methodologies, the concurrent methodology differs in one important respect: the thinking toward the team approach. In the concurrent approach, the focus is on how the team can be most effective and efficient in accomplishing the task or project. There is no effort expended in building team relationships. My experience is that relationship-building exercises should be used only when the team needs to work together over several years or when good relationships are necessary for the team to be successful. For continuous improvement projects in which the duration of the team is relatively short, the focus should be on effective project-management techniques and efficient teaming approaches.

A high-performing team in this context is like a Special Forces team. The team comes together, each member bringing his or her individual skills. As a group, the members train and plan for the specific assignment, then carry out the assignment. When the assignment is completed, they return to their respective bases.

Selection of the team must be done carefully to ensure success. How many people should be on the team? In my experience, the ideal size is five to eight people. If there are fewer than five members, there is rarely enough overall knowledge to bring out the best solutions. If there are more than eight people, the coordination of the team becomes clumsy.

Remember that in this approach you are trying to complete the projects in 90 days, so the emphasis is on accomplishing the task. You are looking for a group that can work reasonably well together for a limited amount of time. You are not looking to build lifelong relationships.

The team leader is the most critical choice. The most important characteristic of the leader is that he or she must have enthusiasm for the project. Enthusiasm is infectious and will rub off on other team members. Next, look for the ability to keep the team on track.

For the rest of the members, you need to make sure that they represent all of the involved functional areas. Look for people who have a good understanding of the process you are trying to fix and that already have an idea of what's working and what's not. Balance the team with detail-oriented people who are prepared to dig for data to better understand what's going on. Try to get people who have a can-do attitude and who are prepared to follow the problem-solving approach. There is no place on the team for a naysayer.

People who are against the process, have an ego, or have something to prove should not be put on the team. They will cause too much distraction.

In the initial period of driving the business improvement process, it's reasonable to ignore those who are against the process or argue against change. Use the advocates to pull the undecided folks off the fence and build the enthusiasm for the process. Don't waste energy trying to deal with the negative people. Pour the energy into the positive people—those people who want to learn and want to change. As the process progresses, more and more folks will come off the fence and join the movement. You will even find that people start to ask when they will get to be on a team, especially as they see kudos and rewards going to the members of the existing teams.

You will need to nip in the bud any destructive behavior or attempts to derail teams. Also, do not allow senior or middle managers to force teams to abandon the rigor of the methodology or to implement pet solutions.

Eventually you will have to deal with those employees who refuse to participate in the process, but do so only after they have had the chance to see the approach and have been given opportunities to alter their behavior. The elements of high-performance teams and how they should be managed will be discussed in detail in chapter 6.

Let's now look at how project selection is refined to ensure that teams are working on value-adding tasks. Earlier I described the criteria for selecting projects, which were:

1. Does the project fit with the strategy?

2. Will the project help to better meet customer needs?

3. Compared with external and internal benchmarks, is the performance trend poor so that there is plenty of room for improvement?

4. Will the project be easy to accomplish?

To ensure that projects meet these criteria, it is necessary to gather data about potential projects and refine the decision making surrounding them. Projects must never be selected on a hunch or because someone thinks it might be a good idea—no matter who that someone might be. Always base the decision on facts. It is absolutely paramount that the projects chosen are proven to meet the criteria. No company can afford the waste of resources or loss of time that results from working on the wrong projects.

An easy method to verify a project's suitability is to run a swift diagnostic across the business, plant, or function in which the project will be run. The diagnostic should ask a series of questions that can flush out the need for, and the potential returns from, a project.

Strategic Direction

- What is the strategy for this unit?
- What are the key performance measures and actual performance?

Customer Needs

- What is market share for this product or service?
- Who are the competitors? What are they doing relative to this company?
- Is technology changing the way business is done?

Business Performance

- What are the financial indicators for this product or service and this unit?
- What are the major expenditure categories?

- What are the general quality measures for scrap, complaints, warranty costs, and so on?

- What are throughput, efficiency, yield, and so on?

Time Measures

- What is the cycle time of the process?

- What are the delivery time and performance?

- What is utilization time of the assets involved?

These questions should not take weeks to answer. The senior manager responsible for the unit should lead the process, supported by his team. The senior manager should involve all applicable functions, ask questions, and gather enough data over a couple of hours to be 80 percent sure of the results, then move to action. The senior manager should not waste time trying for perfection.

As the details of the diagnostic unfurl, then, like a detective trying to solve a murder, you should start to key in on those projects that are the most likely suspects. For example, if the goal is to improve financial performance, is the project hitting the area in which the largest expenditures are? Or, if you are trying to improve overall scrap rates, is the project attacking the largest scrap-generating process?

After all the potential projects are identified, it should be relatively easy to prioritize them based on their potential impacts on strategic direction, customer satisfaction, and performance results. At this point, you should also take into account how difficult the project will be to accomplish. If the number two or number three projects in a particular area can be easily accomplished, do them first. The idea is to find the projects that meet strategic needs and complete as many of them as quickly as possible to provide momentum toward the strategic goals. After the projects are defined, you should set up project teams to attack them and follow the 90-day project methodology to resolution.

THE 90-DAY PROJECT METHODOLOGY

I developed the 90-day methodology over several years while observing what worked well for teams and the major reasons teams failed. It became clear that the successful teams developed a road map to follow for their projects, whereas the unsuccessful teams floundered at each stage, debating what to do next. At one of Bill Conway's "Right Way to Manage" seminars, I learned that all work is part of a process, so I incorporated detailed process mapping as the central tool for gaining understanding of the process before moving to problem solving. The 30-, 60- and 90-day review sessions were added at the prompting of Jean Mauldin, a former boss, who liked to see milestones and reviews to keep the projects on track.

Based on what I learned, I created the 90-day project methodology, which consists of the following steps:

Step 1: Define the Process

- Name the process.
- State the purpose (mission) of the process.
- Identify the output of the process.
- List the customers and partners and define their requirements.
- List the inputs and their suppliers.
- Define the boundaries of the process.
- Identify the connection between the process and external customers.

Step 2: Map the Current Process (Macro View)

- Identify the critical activities in the process.
- Define the sequence of the activities.
- Define the information flow through the system.
- Identify major relationships with other processes.
- Draw a simple diagram that depicts the process.

Step 3: Map the Current Process (Micro View)

- Identify the major subprocesses.
- Define the sequence of the subprocesses.
- Identify activities in each subprocess and their sequences.
- Identify relationships between the subprocesses.
- Draw a map of each subprocess.
- Draw a diagram that shows how the subprocesses are connected.

Step 4: Analyze the Process

- Identify performance measures, such as customer satisfaction, cycle times, costs, variation, and efficiency.

- Collect data to determine how well the process is performing.

- Analyze the data to identify problem areas.

- Prepare graphs that chart the performance.

- Evaluate the approaches and performance of competitors.

- Benchmark the processes of world-class companies.

Step 5: Brainstorm Ways the Process Can Be Changed

- Examine the flowcharts of each process and subprocess to find ways to eliminate unnecessary parts of the process. Ask these questions:

  - What added value does this activity provide?

  - What is actually done or achieved?

  - Why is the activity necessary at all?

  - What else might be done?

- Examine the flowcharts of each process and subprocess to find ways to combine and rearrange operations to be more effective. Ask these questions:

  - Where is this operation being done?

  - Why is the operation done at that particular place?

  - Where else might the operation be done?

- Simplify the operations. Ask these questions:

  - How is the operation done?

  - Why is the operation done that particular way?

  - How else might the operation be done?

- Examine the results of the just-completed analysis and brainstorm further improvements or changes that might be made.

Step 6: Map the New Proposed Process

- Identify the critical activities in the new process.

- Define the new sequence of activities.

- Define the new information flow.

- Identify relationships with other processes.

- Identify the subprocesses and their sequence.

- Draw the macro and micro maps of the new process.

- Get buy-in from involved parties.

- Implement the changes.

Step 7: Control the New Process

- Put an ongoing measurement system in place.

- Document the new procedures.

- Provide training on the new process.

- Put a feedback and control system in place.

- Report on the new process to ensure that everyone is aware of the changes.

The steps are completed in accordance with the timetable given in appendix A. You might think that if the projects are chosen correctly and aligned with the strategic direction of the business, no one can argue with their importance and the need to support them with the required resources. *Wrong!* My experience is that teams are often left to flounder. Senior managers must spell out both the importance and urgency of these projects. By setting a 90-day time line and having 30-day reviews, senior managers show their commitment to these key projects. The team must set an aggressive project plan when faced with 30-day reviews and the need to deliver in 90 days. (Some teams might have a problem that cannot be solved in 90 days. However, my experience with these time lines is that teams deliver much quicker and with better results, rarely taking more than 120 days to reach completion.)

ENDNOTES

1. Thomas J. Peters and Robert H. Waterman Jr., *In Search of Excellence: Lessons from America's Best-Run Companies* (New York: Warner Books, 1988).
2. Thomas J. Peters, "System + Passion + Persistence = Quality Revolution," TomPeters!Company (www.tompeters.com).

5

Ingredient 4: Basic Training

A SIMPLE TRAINING REVIEW ACROSS THE WHOLE BUSINESS

In my experience, I have found that it is important to fill the fundamental training gaps that might exist in an organization. I have found that basic skills are often not well established. Sometimes tasks are taught by example, such as an operator watching another operator perform a task, with no standards or testing.

I was responsible for a manufacturing plant on the Texas–Mexico border, where managers were having tremendous problems with operator turnover. Many of the new employees would go through basic training for 12 weeks. When they were put into the shift system, they would leave after a few weeks of rotation. The HR specialist examined the situation and concluded that although they were receiving adequate training on how to operate the machines, they were not being exposed to the full spectrum of their duties, including cleaning and quality testing. These skills were generally taught by other operators after they started their shift rotation. Generally, the employees found it difficult to cope and became stressed with the sudden increase in perceived duties. They would quit and look for an easier job.

The HR specialist modified the training, put the new trainees on shifts earlier in the training process, exposed them up front to all of the work, and implemented testing to determine whether they had the ability to cope. Under this scheme, only fully competent operators who were successfully tested in all areas of the job were transferred to the shift roster. The turnover issue was eliminated.

People generally have poor knowledge of the products they make and of the overall production processes, so they do not understand how their job impacts other areas of the business. For example, in this same manufacturing plant, there was also a quality issue: operator inspections were not being carried out well and the rejection rate by customers was high. The operators made electrical wire. To them, it was simply spools of wire. They had no knowledge of how the wire was being used. By bringing products that used the wire to meetings—products that many families used, such as electric hand tools, washing machine motors, and starters and alternators for cars—and spending just an hour briefing the workforce about the important role that the wire played in those products, the operators became motivated and the quality levels improved.

The same applies to service situations. Frequently, people who interact with customers are given little training in how to ask the right questions, make appropriate comments, or deal with delicate situations. Time and effort needs to be expended to make sure that all employees better understand how their jobs fit into the big picture and how service errors can result in customer issues or even lost business. For example, in one corporate office, employees preparing invoices were oblivious to the fact that small errors or delays in customers' invoices resulted in the company not being paid for an additional month. After making the accounts payable group aware of the overall process being used by some very large customers, the staff concentrated on issuing invoices with fewer errors. The company's cash flow improved by $1 million.

Promotions are often made without providing extra training. As a result, some supervisors and managers have poor organization, task-management, and delegation skills.

By finding and correcting the training gaps, significant improvement can be achieved in organizational performance. You need to make sure that the workforce has been properly trained in basic skills before you provide training in business improvement skills. A review should be made covering the following areas:

1. Safety

   - Does every employee know the safety aspects of their job?

   - Are Occupational Safety and Health Administration (OSHA) requirements being complied with?

2. Task accomplishment

   - Has everyone been trained in the tasks they are expected to do?

   - Are there standards and tests that ensure compliance?

3. Product knowledge

   - Is there a basic product training program so that everyone knows what the company does or makes?

   - Is there an advanced product training program for those who need it?

4. Work process

   - Does everyone understand how their job fits into the overall production or service process?

   - In the office area, does everyone understand the basic cash flow cycle and how the tasks they accomplish can affect it?

5. Customers' needs

   - Does the sales force carry the flag for customers?

   - Are customers' wants documented and available to those employees who supply product or service?

   - Does everyone recognize the benefit of working to satisfy both internal and external customers?

6. Management and supervisory skills

   - Has time management been taught to managers and supervisors?

   - Do managers and supervisors know the basics of handling and motivating people?

   - Have all managers and supervisors received basic project management training?

After the training gaps are identified, they can be incorporated into the first-year training program along with the business improvement skills. The training to correct shortcomings in the areas I just described should be short, simple, and as hands-on as possible. I am not talking about sending employees to extended off-site courses. You should encourage your own HR group or departmental managers to put these courses together and deliver them in the workplace as quickly and efficiently as they can. One of the major roles of a manager is to train the people who work for them.

THE ESSENTIAL BASIC TOOLBOX

In chapter 4, I mentioned that, like apprentices, team members should start by learning how to use the basic tools before trying to use any of the advanced tools. To participate in several waves of 90-day projects, team members only need to learn about and use the STOP process, process mapping, the seven simple statistical tools, and problem-solving techniques.

THE STOP PROCESS

In chapter 2, I introduced you to the STOP process. Because this process is integral to the Recipe, let's revisit that process.

Start with yourself and ask the following questions:

1. What are your roles and responsibilities? Include your:

   - Job functions

   - Major goals

   - Key tasks

2. How do you accomplish these? Include the:

   - Tasks you do

   - Tasks you delegate

   - Meetings you attend

   - Reports you write and receive

3. What can you change? Include any task you can:

   - Eliminate

   - Combine

   - Simplify

Appendix F provides some worksheets that you can use to record your answers. When you are completing the worksheets, keep asking the questions: How does this add value? How does this fit with the vision, mission, and goals that are set?

After you have finished the STOP process, repeat the exercise with your team. Ask each individual to go through the questions and share their answers with the rest of the team.

PROCESS MAPPING

Process mapping is the technique of identifying the events that occur in a process and recording them on paper in as much detail as possible. By going through this exercise, a team can come to a common understanding of what is occurring in a process. This knowledge helps the team identify missing information that it needs to collect in order to make informed decisions about how to modify the process. As I mentioned previously, the preferred process-mapping method is to draw the map on flipchart-sized paper that can be put up on the wall during team sessions so that it can be easily referred to in discussions. The steps in drawing the map are:

1. Map the current process at the macro level.

   - Identify the critical activities (only major or core activities at this point).

   - Define the order in which these activities occur.

   - Draw as simple a picture as possible to represent the process.

   - Get everyone to review the map and modify it until everyone agrees it represents what is occurring in the process.

2. Add the process details to the map.

   - Add the major subprocesses.

   - For each subprocess, answer these questions:

     – What is being done?

     – When is it being done?

     – Where is it being done?

     – Who is doing it?

     – How is it being done?

     – How long does it take?

Figure 5.1   Gaining an understanding of a process through process mapping.

The answers to many of these questions may not be clear and data will have to be gathered to adequately understand what is happening—therein lies the power of the technique. In many instances, there are different perceptions of what is happening in a process. Process mapping prompts the team to gather information to reveal the facts, which brings an understanding of the process by all team members, as Figure 5.1 shows. By putting the process map together, the team gains a common perspective, which aids in problem solving.

After the map is complete, the team can start to gather the rest of the information needed about the process before starting the analysis. This information includes data about inputs and their suppliers; outputs and the customers they go to; satisfaction levels; cycle times; delays and where they occur; and scrap and other wastes. When possible, the data should be entered directly on the map.

SEVEN SIMPLE STATISTICAL TOOLS

Let's now look at the seven simple statistical tools that are used to gather and analyze data. The first tool is the *run chart,* which is depicted in Figure 5.2. A run chart is a line plot of values measured over time. It is used to identify how the process measure fluctuates over a given time period. It can indicate trends, shifts, or cycles that might be occurring. It can also be used to compare the output from two or more similar processes or machines by plotting the output from each on the same graph, which makes the comparison easier.

To prepare a run chart, follow these steps:

1. Decide on the property that will be charted.

2. Gather at least 20 to 25 data points. The number of points captured should represent a reasonable period of the process, such as several days of production or 20 days of invoices.

3. Create a graph with the vertical axis representing the value and the horizontal axis representing the sequence or time of capture of the data points.

4. Plot the data on the graph.

5. Analyze the data. Look for trends or patterns that appear.

The second tool is the *histogram,* which is depicted in Figure 5.3. A histogram is a bar chart of the process variable distribution. It shows how frequently each value occurs.

Studying a histogram plot of a variable can provide much information about the process. It can tell you where the process is centered. By placing the specification limits on the graph, you can see actual performance relative to the desired performance. The shape of the distribution also indicates issues with the process.

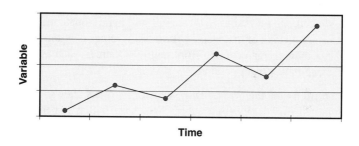

Figure 5.2 Run chart.

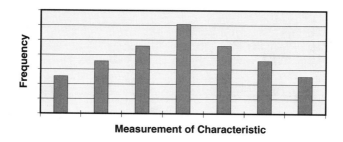

Figure 5.3 Histogram.

To prepare a histogram, follow these steps:

1. Decide on the variable to be plotted.

2. Gather data, generally a minimum of 50 data points. The data gathered should cover a reasonable period of output from the process, such as a week's worth of invoices.

3. Decide on the class intervals to be plotted. For instance, if the lowest value is 1 and the highest value is 50, you can split the data into five intervals of 10 values: 1 to 10, 11 to 20, 21 to 30, 31 to 40, and 41 to 50. Or, you can split the data into 10 intervals of five values: 1 to 5, 6 to 10, 11 to 15, and so on. My preference is to try to use eight to 12 intervals for histogram plots.

4. Create the graph with the horizontal axis showing the intervals and the vertical axis showing the frequency of occurrence.

5. Plot the data on the graph.

6. Analyze the chart. Look at the shape. Is it a bell-shaped curve, which indicates a normal distribution? If the curve is bell shaped, the tallest bar in the center will approximate the average value of the process. Two or more peaks in the plot can indicate data coming from multiple sources, such as two machines or two operators.

The third tool is the *Pareto chart,* which Figure 5.4 shows. The Pareto chart is named after the Pareto principle, which states that 20 percent of the causes create 80 percent of the problems. A Pareto chart is used to rank-order issues and identify where to prioritize activities.

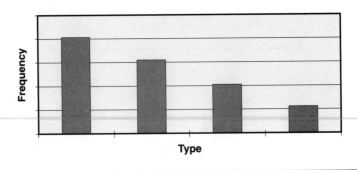

Figure 5.4 Pareto chart.

To prepare a Pareto chart, follow these steps:

1. Decide on the property that will be charted, such as scrap or rejected invoices.

2. Decide on the categories or type of problems that will be logged. For example, the categories for rejected invoices might be: incorrect price, wrong quantity, does not match order, and so forth.

3. Gather data. Enough data should be gathered to be representative of the process, such as a month's worth of invoices.

4. Prepare a graph with the frequencies on the vertical axis and the type or category on the horizontal axis.

5. Plot the data. Put the largest frequency first, second largest next, and so on.

6. Analyze the data. The largest problem is the one that should be worked on first.

Second-level pareto charts should be prepared when necessary to drill down into the data and guide activity to the most critical area. For example, to analyze the scrap for a particular production unit that makes several products, you might need to create one Pareto chart that shows which product generates the most scrap, and then create a second Pareto chart that shows the causes of that scrap.

The fourth tool is the *flowchart,* which Figure 5.5 illustrates. The flowchart is a mini process map. It graphically depicts a portion of the process to

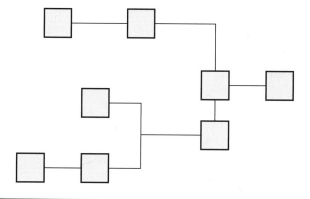

Figure 5.5   Flowchart.

aid understanding. It is used to identify specific activities within the process. These are:

- Decision points, which are represented by a diamond

- Inspection points, which are represented by a square

- Operations, which are represented by a circle

- Movement or transportation, which is represented by an arrow

- Delays, which are represented by the letter D

- Storage, which is represented by an inverted triangle

To prepare a flowchart, follow these steps:

1. Identify the activities.

2. Define the order in which they occur.

3. Draw as simple a picture as possible to represent the process.

4. Identify the type of activity for each step in the process and insert the appropriate icon in the flowchart. For example, Figure 5.6 shows the icons for each step of the following drill process:

   - Step 1: Start machine.

   - Step 2: Insert blank.

   - Step 3:Drill.

   - Step 4: Inspect hole.

   - Step 5: If the hole is bad, go to step 6. If the hole is good, go to step 7.

   - Step 6: Redrill.

   - Step 7: Store.

Figure 5.6 Sample flowchart for a drill process.

The fifth tool is the *correlation chart,* which Figure 5.7 shows. The correlation chart, which is also called a scatter diagram, is used to study the relationship between two variables. It is particularly useful to compare the effect an input variable has on an output variable.

To prepare a correlation chart, follow these steps:

1. Decide which variables you are going to compare.

2. Gather the data for each variable. It is important that the data is gathered as matching pairs. For example, if you are comparing height versus weight of people, you would measure the height and weight of each individual and record that data as a pair of values (height, weight).

3. Prepare a graph with the values for variable 1 on the vertical axis and the values for variable 2 on the horizontal axis. For example, in the chart comparing height versus weight, the height values would go on the vertical axis and the weight values would go on the horizontal axis.

4. Plot each pair of data on the graph. The point goes where the values intersect.

5. After all points are plotted, examine the chart. If there is high correlation, the points will fall close to a line that can be inserted in the middle of the points. If there is no correlation, the points will be scattered all over the place, with no apparent pattern.

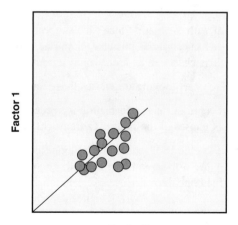

Factor 2

Figure 5.7 Correlation chart.

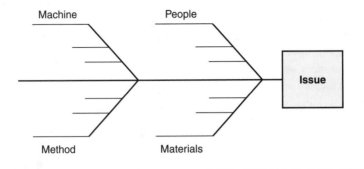

Figure 5.8   Fishbone diagram.

The sixth tool is the *fishbone diagram,* which Figure 5.8 illustrates. The fishbone diagram, which is also called the cause-and-effect diagram, is used to create a snapshot of the collective knowledge of a group about a problem. By graphically representing the potential causes, this diagram allows the team to reach consensus on what aspects need further study in order to define the root cause of an issue.

To prepare a fishbone diagram, follow these steps:

1. On a flipchart, draw a diagram similar to that in Figure 5.8.

2. Agree on the problem statement and write it into the box. Make sure that the statement is as specific as possible by defining what, where, and when. For example, the problem statement might read, "High scrap rate on machine 3 when making product B."

3. Brainstorm with the team. Place each suggestion on the chart trying to be as specific as possible. Continue until all ideas are recorded. The chart can be redrawn once completed if needed.

4. Analyze the chart looking for causes that occur in multiple areas.

5. Decide where additional information is needed to clarify which are the root causes of the issue. (There might be more than one.)

An alternative method to generate a fishbone diagram is to place a bare-bones chart in the work area being studied. Then ask everyone to add their input to the fishbone diagram.

The last tool is the *control chart,* which is depicted in Figure 5.9.

Control charts are used to monitor process variables over time, according to a series of statistical rules. They are a special form of the run chart.

The type of control chart used depends on the type of data being gathered. There are two types of data: variables measured on a continuous scale

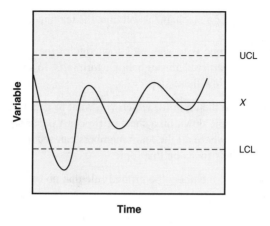

Figure 5.9 Control chart.

(such as temperature) and attributes counted as discrete events (such as the number of shipping errors). For each of the data types, there are several potential chart types.

Essentially the charts are a time series plot similar to the run chart, except that a line representing the average value (x) and lines representing the upper control limit (UCL) and the lower control limit (LCL) are added to the chart. The UCL and LCL are calculated from a statistical analysis of the first 25 to 30 points on the chart. The control limits and a series of rules concerning where a series of points fall are used to make minor adjustments to the process and identify special causes of variation. There are several software programs that can be used to prepare control charts. Two that I have used are PQ Systems' SQCpack and Minitab.

PROBLEM-SOLVING TECHNIQUES

Teams can use several problem-solving techniques. The first technique I always like to remind teams to use is BCS (basic common sense). You should keep the problem-solving process as simple as possible by telling teams to look for those solutions that make sense.

The second problem-solving technique is to find someone with expertise in the problem area and ask that person what he or she would do. The team members will have many ideas, but they must be encouraged and coached to seek expert advice when it is available. If the team's project involves motivating people, the team members should ask the HR group. If the team is looking for a mechanical solution, the team members should ask an engineer.

The third technique is to use the knowledge of the team. Frequently, this knowledge is gathered through brainstorming. To conduct a brainstorming session, follow these steps:

1. Clearly state the topic for which you want to generate ideas. Write the topic down on a sheet of flipchart paper and pin it on the wall where all the team members can see it so that they maintain their focus on that topic.

2. Tell the team members the ground rule that no comment or criticism of any idea is permitted.

3. Allocate five to 10 minutes for people to think quietly about the topic.

4. Begin to collect the ideas by having one person state one idea. After that person states one idea, have the person next to him or her state one idea, and so on. It's okay for someone to pass, and rejoin later, if he or she does not have an idea.

5. A scribe should accurately record the ideas for all to see on the flipchart. As each page is filled, stick it on the wall so that it's in view for everyone. In some cases, two scribes and two flipcharts might be needed to keep up with the flow of ideas.

6. Keep going until all ideas are exhausted.

7. When all of the ideas have been recorded, take five minutes to clarify ideas and to eliminate duplications.

8. Make sure a record of all ideas is retained for potential future use.

The fourth problem-solving technique is the *is/is not matrix*. This simple tool helps clarify what, where, when, how, and who when a problem has occurred. The matrix also helps identify common themes when a problem is recurring.

By filling out the is/is not matrix, you can sift through data like a detective sifting through clues in a murder case. As Figure 5.10 shows, it is much easier to analyze information when it is laid out in such a format. The matrix in Figure 5.10 was filled out to discover why one particular line in a sweater plant was producing many defects. In this case, the cause of the problem was the transfer of an operator to a machine with which he was

	Is	Is Not	Therefore
Where (The physical or geographic location of the event)	Line 2	Lines 1, 3, 4, and 5	Equipment differences? *Machine 2 is the oldest and has different setup.* Material differences? *Raw materials the same.*
When (Hour, day, week, or month the event occurs; relationship to other events— before, during, or after)	In first two hours of the third shift	First shift or second shift	Operator dependent? Training? Shift changeover?
What and How	50 percent defective units in first two hours	Fewer than five percent defects	Machine, time, or operator dependent?
Who	Newly assigned operator transferred from days; only one third shift supervisor	Two supervisors on first and second shifts	Does the supervisor have time to deal with problems? *Deals with schedule for first two hours.* Operator skill level? *Operator does not understand setup on this machine.*

Figure 5.10 Is/is not matrix for defective sweaters on knitting line.

unfamiliar. The supervisor had duties to cover and could not assist the new operator for the first few hours to help in resetting the machine. A short training session for the operator solved the problem.

The fifth problem-solving technique is the *five whys,* which is depicted in Figure 5.11. To get to the root cause of a problem, ask "Why?" at least five times. Consider the following example:

"The reactor overheated." Why?

"Because the water flow dropped." Why?

Figure 5.11   The five whys.

"Because one of the pumps stopped." Why?

"Because the bearing failed." Why?

"Because the bearing had not been lubricated." Why?

"The lubrication guy was on vacation and no one covered for him."

Eventually the root cause of the problem is discovered. A solution can now be found that addresses this root cause rather than just the symptoms of the problem. In this example, solutions might include installing an automatic lubrication system or having the supervisor schedule replacements during vacation periods.

With process mapping, the seven simple statistical tools and the five problem-solving techniques, teams can start on the path to process improvement.

I cannot overemphasize the need to keep reminding teams to keep things simple. They need to keep asking "Why?" until they reach a satisfactory answer. They also need to keep asking "Does this make sense?" The ideal solution will.

6

Ingredient 5:
Managed Teams

WINNING TEAMS ARE COACHED
TO SUCCESS

When you examine the record books of teams that won the Super Bowl, you will not find statistics about how well the teams got along with each other or how often the teams stuck to their agenda. Instead, you will find statistics about how many points the teams scored compared to their opponents. In the NFL, teams and their coaches remain intact only if they win.

The same holds true in the business arena. Leadership teams stay intact only if their companies are profitable. Like NFL teams, business improvement teams' performance is not measured by the members' ability to get along with each other or their ability to stick to meeting agendas. The teams' performance is measured by such statistics as how often they meet their goals and whether they do so within the required period of time.

In the 90-day project methodology that I advocate, the focus is on enabling teams to effectively and efficiently meet their goals in as short a period of time as possible. There is no effort expended in building team relationships other than those absolutely necessary to succeed.

Good teams usually have good coaches. In the case of business improvement teams, the role of coach falls to the sponsor. In my experience, the best business improvement teams usually include a senior manager who takes on the role of mentor and coach, and helps them through the process.

The Recipe emphasizes managing the team process to maximize the potential for success. Team members are expected to come together, follow the process, work together both during and outside of team meetings, and accomplish the task. They are not expected to like each other, become the best of friends, or socialize, so no time is spent on team development activities.

Each member is selected for the knowledge and experience he or she brings to the team—the person's individuality is desired. The business improvement team mechanism needs to ensure that the group can reach agreement when necessary and not have dysfunctional behavior that disrupts the process. That is all.

Other approaches often incorporate two or three days of team training to make sure that team members get acquainted, understand each other's personality traits, and clearly understand the roles and behaviors expected of them. My experience is that true behavior change takes months or, in some cases, years. Because the improvement team is challenged to deliver results in 90 days, this type of training has little impact on short-term team behavior. Thus, a better approach is to manage the team through the process for the duration of the project.

I do advocate a team development approach for groups that have to work together over long periods of time, such as leadership teams and departmental teams. However, my experience is that development approaches still must be tempered with project goals. In many cases, I have seen that it is sufficient for team members to become merely tolerant of each other as long as they are prepared to work together. They do not have to be a cohesive group that also plays together.

If you want a collaborative workplace that honors diversity and that values the differences individuals bring to the organization, you need to put in place an organization development program to achieve that end. Put all workers through Myers-Briggs training so that they better understand their colleagues.[1] You need to weed out the dysfunctional players from the workplace right away. Don't wait until they show that behavior on an improvement team. They exhibit the bad behavior every day if it's in their character. Above all, have a management development program to ensure that leaders, managers, and supervisors model the behavior you want.

CHARACTERISTICS OF HIGH-PERFORMANCE BUSINESS IMPROVEMENT TEAMS

High-performance business improvement teams exhibit the following characteristics:

1. They follow the methodology to ensure success.

2. They have the ability to stay focused on the objective.

3. They use each team member's talents.

4. They are able to work together for the duration of the project.

5. They devote the time needed to bring the project to fruition in 90 days.

6. They hold meetings efficiently. (They have agendas and clear objectives for each meeting, they stick to the agenda, and they do what's needed during the meeting.)

7. They do the work that's needed between meetings.

8. They allow constructive disagreement to bring out the best solutions.

9. They communicate issues to and from their colleagues in the workplace to broaden the knowledge applied to the issue.

10. They encourage others outside the team to support the team when needed.

11. They have the collective will to make change happen.

Managers often intuitively perceive that the leader of any project should have many of these characteristics. This leads to repetitive selection of the same group of leaders over and over again for projects. Look deeper when selecting teams: you are trying to develop and expose all team members to these concepts. Some members will evolve into capable leaders.

Every team must have a sponsor. The ideal sponsor is the manager of the department in which the project is occurring. That manager has the authority to change the rules and work methods in that department, so he or she is a powerful enabler for the team. In addition, the manager should have most of the skills needed to help the team be successful. If the manager cannot be the sponsor for some dire reason, then look to that person's boss to step in, or a manager from another department. By having managers as the sponsors, you are showing their commitment and involvement, which reflects the importance of the projects.

In large companies, the role of sponsor is often handed to a specific group, such as the quality or Six Sigma department, or to outside consultants. Although it's fine to use these groups for training and facilitation, the business improvement process and teams must be owned by the company. Managers own what is happening in their departments, so they must devote the time to overseeing the business improvement projects. They should view it as part of their everyday work.

THE 10-STEP PROCESS FOR MANAGING TEAMS

There is a 10-step process for managing teams that sponsors need to follow:

1. Make sure you understand the 90-day project methodology so that you can help the team follow it.

2. Select the team members to make sure that the team has the talent it needs. Choose the leader carefully because he or she will be your ambassador.

3. Make sure the objective of the team is clear. Prepare the charter for the team and meet with the team in its opening session to ensure clarity.

4. Ensure that the STOP process is completed for the team and that the team has the time needed for success.

5. Help the team members to work together. Monitor the pulse of the team and help them overcome difficulties.

6. Help the team understand how to hold effective meetings.

7. Make sure that the work is being completed between meetings. Know what assignments are being delegated by the team and track them as part of your everyday work.

8. Help the team members reach consensus. Guide them on how to make decisions and how to make disagreements constructive.

9. Keep the door open for communication with colleagues and for controlled use of external resources for the team.

10. Help the team see the process through. The 30- and 60-day reviews should be working sessions in which you not only check on the team's progress but also help the team identify problems and ways to overcome them.

At the end of the process, the sponsor has the added responsibility of making sure that the team's work is adequately recognized and rewarded. Before I discuss that responsibility in chapter 7, let's delve into the details of what is needed at each of the 10 steps.

Step 1: Understanding the 90-Day Project Methodology

Here the onus is on the sponsor to be sure that he or she understands the overall 90-day project methodology well enough to be able to assess whether the team is on track to meet its goals or whether he or she needs to intervene to increase the activity going on in the project. Sponsors should study the outline of the 90-day project methodology in chapter 4 so that they know the sequence of activities. They shouldn't allow deviation because the methodology works if it's followed.

In the first 30 days, the team should complete the first three steps. The team should have the process well defined and mapped out in significant detail. The team should be actively gathering data to support its understanding of what's happening in the process being improved. By the sixth week, the team should be moving into the problem-solving stage and starting to raise ideas on what can be changed in the process. By the 60-day review, the team should be starting to test some of its ideas. In the last two or three weeks, the team should be making changes in the process where needed and implementing their solutions.

Step 2: Selecting the Team

The ideal size of the team is five to eight members. Smaller teams work faster, but it is essential to make sure that enough knowledge and experience is bought to the team to enable it to find good, permanent solutions to issues.

The team should consist of people who are excited to be involved. Choose the leader carefully because he or she is critical to the successful outcome of the project. This person has to be enthusiastic about the project and happy to be chosen as the leader. The essential skills that the leader needs are the ability to manage tasks, to hold people to deadlines, and to make sure tasks are being completed between meetings. The leader also needs people skills so that he or she can ensure all the people on the team are heard and involved.

A major role of the sponsor is to coach the behavior of the leader in the team environment. The sponsor must assume the role of mentor to the team leader. The sponsor should meet regularly with the team leader to discuss how things are going and to generally help the leader become a better manager of people and tasks.

Sometimes it's better to use a team of one—that is, have the project completed by an individual rather than a team. Circumstances in which this might be applicable are:

- When very specific expertise is required (for example, you need a software engineer to write a computer program to transfer data into a database).

- When the team has completed its work and you need a project manager to implement the solution.

Step 3: Make Sure the Objective Is Clear

The best way to ensure that the team members clearly understand what's expected of them is to put it in writing in a team charter. As Figure 6.1 shows, the charter spells out:

- What process or problem is being studied

- The specific goal of the project

- Any boundaries, including limitations to ensure compliance with safety and environmental standards

- The start date and target finish date

- Who is on the team (sponsor, leader, and team members)

- Dates for the 30-, 60- and 90-day reviews

After the charter is written, it should be given to the leader and each member of the team. The sponsor should attend the first team meeting to check understanding and answer questions the team might have.

This step is a critical milestone. I have observed many teams working hard on the wrong problem because this step was not completed well.

Step 4: Ensure the STOP Process Is Completed for the Team

One of the major reasons for having the department manager be the sponsor for a team is that he or she has the authority to permit activities to be stopped or delayed while the project goes on. The department manager should run the STOP process for the team members and their supervisors. That way, decisions can be made right there and then to cull unnecessary non-value-added work, and everyone is fully aware of what's been decided.

Team members are often enthusiastic about the STOP process because they have the chance to point out and eliminate those activities they have considered wasteful for some time. My experience is that if the STOP

Recipe Company—Team Charter	
Project title	Reduce invoice errors for major customer Johnson Brothers.
Sponsor	Joe Smith
Leader	Mary Jones
Members	Ellen, Tom, and Debbie
Project goal	Reduce invoice errors that are causing Johnson Brothers to delay payment by an average 20 days and bring payments back to an on-time status.
Deliverables	Process changes that will essentially eliminate invoicing errors Changes that can be applied across all customers. Report that can be circulated to other divisions.
Key performance measures	Number of days payment overdue. Number of errors on invoices.
Boundaries	Changes to computer software need department manager's approval. Changes to how the work group handles invoices needs agreement from all involved and supervisor. Changes in staffing roles needs department manager's approval.
Critical dates	Start date: 1/2 30-day review: 2/3 60-day review: 3/5 Target finish date: 4/5

Figure 6.1　Sample team charter.

process is done with an open mind, many non-value-added activities can be eliminated, freeing up the needed time for the team.

Step 5: Help the Team to Work Together

The sponsor should attend team meetings in the early weeks to view the team's performance. However, he or she should be careful not to take control of a meeting or the project. The sponsor needs to attend the meetings as a facilitator or observer and make that clear to the group. The sponsor should make it a point to stay for only a short time, so that their presence doesn't close down the meeting. If the sponsor has any improvements to offer, he or she should do so during a coaching session with the leader.

If a team is struggling, a facilitator specifically trained to help teams function better can be brought in. However, make it clear to the facilitator that he or she must follow the 90-day process closely.

Having the sponsor touch base with team members as they work on delegated tasks outside of team meetings and giving them encouragement on an individual basis can work wonders for the motivation of the team. However, the sponsor needs to be careful not to change or redirect, only encourage, the team members.

Step 6: Help the Team Understand How to Hold Effective Meetings

We've all been to meetings in which we wondered what we're doing there. We've all waited 10 minutes for the stragglers to roll in or, worse, been the late arrival and wasted a lot of collective time. We've all sat and listened as the leader got sidetracked and took the proceedings somewhere they were never meant to go. We've all observed the intransigent arguments of two opinionated colleagues who refused to see each other's point of view, thereby holding the rest of the participants hostage. And we've all left meetings wondering what was decided.

Meetings, however, do not have to be like that. High-performance teams hold high-performance meetings by following the sequence: plan, run, finish, and follow up.

Plan

- Determine the purpose of the meeting.

- Write objectives.

- Determine and list agenda items in sequence.

- Set approximate time for each agenda item.

- Set approximate time limit for whole meeting.

- Schedule best date, time, and location for meeting.

- Send a note to all attendees that specifies the meeting's date, time, and location and that outlines the meeting's purpose, objectives, and preparations needed.

Run

- Start the meeting on time.

- Put the meeting's objectives on a flipchart for all to see.

- Agree on the meeting's agenda and sequence. Change where needed.

- Encourage active participation and open communication.

- Be flexible with the agenda. Allow plenty of discussion but do not allow the group to get sidetracked. Refer to the objectives when necessary.

- Encourage the group to reach consensus on issues.

- Capture ideas and issues that are not relevant to the meeting agenda on a "parking lot board" to be dealt with later.

Finish

- If no consensus is reached on an issue, define what has been agreed to and hold the decision for the next meeting.

- Agree and write down what actions will be taken.

- For each action, define *what, how, when,* and by *whom.*

- Set objectives, date, time, and location for next meeting.

Follow Up

- Have the leader check in with those meeting participants who have work to do between meetings to make sure they understand and accomplish the task in time for the next meeting.

- Issue a written summary of the meeting to all participants (nothing fancy—handwritten bullet points are fine).

- Prepare for the next meeting.

Step 7: Make Sure the Work Is Being Completed between Meetings

It's not what happens in a team meeting that determines the fate of a team, but rather what happens between meetings. This is true for all teams, not just business improvement teams. When any team meets, the team members should be able to have open, honest discussions about the topics they are reviewing and be able to trust other team members to keep the discussions in the meeting room. If members disparage colleagues or the proceedings back in the workplace, they destroy the fabric of the team and undermine its activities. Sponsors need to keep any such behavior in check.

If members of a business improvement team fail to do assignments allotted to them, they let down the whole team. It's important that a strong commitment to being part of the team is made by all team members and that everyone pulls their weight. Sponsors need to encourage and motivate team members to keep their commitments. Sponsors also need to ensure a balance is being maintained between the members' team-related tasks and their normal job duties. A good way to ensure this balance is to have each supervisor recognize the project as part of the team members' daily work and report on the project activities in daily or weekly review meetings. That way, supervisors treat the projects with the importance needed and they do not assign team members too much work after the members return from team meetings. Sponsors merely need to ask the supervisors to support the team projects, which is why department managers make the best sponsors. They are in the ideal position to balance daily and project work and ensure all tasks are completed.

Step 8: Help the Team Members Reach Consensus

In business improvement teams, there are five ways a decision can be made:

- The team members can reach consensus.
- The team members can reach a compromise.
- There can be a majority vote.
- The leader can decide.
- The sponsor can decide.

Consensus is finding a decision that every team member can live with, buy into, and support. No member opposes the decision.

Compromise generally involves team members with opposing viewpoints making concessions so that some middle ground is reached. Sometimes people might be unhappy with the decision, but they accept it as best they can.

Majority vote is the standard democratic method. The team members vote on the issue, and the majority rules. It's not uncommon for team members to use this method when they're prioritizing items because it keeps the prioritization process moving along.

Leader and sponsor decisions are both management decisions. They are unilateral in that input need not be taken from other people.

The ideal way to make a decision for important issues is to reach consensus. However, a consensus is not necessary for every decision. You don't need to have a two-hour discussion about when to take a 10-minute break—

the team leader can just decide. Some decisions might have to be made by the sponsor. For example, the sponsor must make the decisions about issues that are outside the boundaries set for the team.

In order to avoid confusion for the team, the sponsor should give guidance to the team early on about what type of decisions to expect and which decisions must be referred to the sponsor. The sponsor should clarify that the major role of the team leader is to manage the project; therefore, commonsense decisions concerning the process should be made by the leader. The leader, in turn, might decide to accept a majority vote or compromise. However, the team must use the consensus method for items of major importance.

Teams should use the following process for reaching consensus:

1. Clearly state the decision to be made, then write it down and post it for all to see.

2. Explore the choices.

3. Involve everyone in the discussion and listen to every point of view.

4. If one person is against a particular decision, ask that person to express his or her point of view to the group, trying to persuade the others to change.

5. Repeat the process with a person who has a different point of view.

6. After all arguments are presented, take a simple hand vote.

7. If the vote is not unanimous, ask someone from the minority to review the advantages of his or her decision.

8. Have someone from the majority reiterate the advantages of the that decision.

9. Repeat the vote.

10. If the vote is not unanimous, ask the minority what it would take to change their point of view.

11. Ask the same of the majority.

12. Keep the discussion open until consensus is reached and everyone buys in and supports the final decision.

If the process is taking a lot longer than the time allotted in the meeting agenda, the decision can be deferred. However, it is preferable to see the process through once it's started.

Always remember to have each side present its case. On more than one occasion, I have seen the minority persuade the majority to change their decision once they clearly understood each other's viewpoints.

Step 9: Keep the Door Open for Communication with Colleagues and for Controlled Use of External Resources

The sponsor should encourage team members to keep their colleagues informed about what is happening with the project. In essence, the team members represent everyone in the business and should be openly reporting back to and soliciting input from the workforce. A good method is to post the minutes of team meetings or a summary of each project's status for all to see. Unless a particular project is of a truly sensitive nature, such as a breakthrough new product that might be patented, open reporting is to be advocated. Often great ideas will come from employees who are not on the team when people know that open communication and involvement are encouraged. Encouraging open communication and involvement also motivates others to join teams in the next round of projects.

Team members should be permitted to ask for help. If they feel someone's expertise is needed, they can co-opt that person for a meeting or particular task. However, do not permit the team to grow in number during its lifetime. Keep it to the original size.

If the team members need training, then give it to them. Try to make any training part of their working sessions. For instance, if the team members need training on plotting data, have the training coincide with the data-plotting meeting so they can learn and apply the new skills at the same time. Learning and doing is the most effective type of training.

If the team members need help with facilitation, then give it to them. Pair facilitators with leaders so that the leader gains maximum benefit and skills from the experience.

In all of these cases, make the point that these resources are also part of the learning experience. After the team learns the new skills, they will be better equipped for future projects.

Step 10: Help the Team See the Process Through

The 30- and 60-day review sessions should not be simple information transfers. If the department manager has been adequately fulfilling the sponsor role, he or she will already have a reasonable idea of how the project is going.

The sponsor should use the review as an opportunity for an open working session with the team. As the sponsor, try to find out what problems the team members are facing and whether they might need help to resolve those problems. Review the process maps and graphical data they have prepared to make sure what they've done is not flawed in any way. Listen to the team members' ideas about potential solutions and make sure those solutions are implementable. Remember, the role of the sponsor is to help the team be successful.

If a senior manager is present at a review, the sponsor should help the team members present their work and communicate their information and ideas. Encourage the senior manager to provide praise when possible.

At the final project meeting, the sponsor needs to help the team prepare its presentation. Once again, encourage the senior managers to give praise to the team and recognize its activities.

One final activity for the sponsor is to extend the time allotted for the project beyond 90 days, if needed. There are some projects that genuinely need more time to complete and are worthy of an extension. However, most projects can be successfully completed within the 90 days if these 10 steps for managing teams are followed.

EXAMPLES OF WINNING TEAMS

There are many skeptics who will say that significant projects cannot be completed in a 90-day time frame or that this approach to using teams without significant development training will not be successful. I have witnessed many teams make incredible changes in even shorter periods of time by using the methods I just described. One such team improved the output of material used for the production of power plants by 50 percent during a two-month period in November and December 1999.

Faced with a booming market, the production unit was extending lead times to meet customer demand. Output was running at 600 units per month. The sales force said it could sell 900 units per month if manufacturing could improve production. The senior managers' first thoughts were to buy an additional production line, but they soon discovered the line would take 12 months to install. So, a team was chartered to increase output by any method possible. Within three weeks the team had identified all the causes of lost production and started implementing changes to eliminate these causes. By the end of the first month, production was up to 750 units per month, and after just 60 days, the target of 900 units was met.

In the fourth month, a record number of units were produced—more than 1000—and the sales force was being pushed to sell more. The production of more than 900 units per month was sustained for more than six months until the market started to recede. The increase in earnings from all the additional sales was significant, and the capital to add an additional production line was never spent, which meant a savings of more than $2 million.

The 90-day project methodology works on the service side of business also. For example, a customer service team was challenged to improve on-time deliveries to a major customer from 70 percent to more than 95 percent in three months or face a major loss of business. The main problem was that the deliveries were made by rail, and this mode of transportation was chronically unreliable. The VP of sales was convinced that the only way to save the business was to put consignment stock at every one of the customer's locations at a cost of several million dollars to cash flow.

Before taking that drastic measure, the senior managers chartered the customer service team to look for alternatives. Within 20 days, the team had come up with a solution—to put a small number of railcars on spurs close to the customers' sites. When railcars were lost in the railroad system, these standby railcars could be pulled in on short notice to meet the customer's delivery time. By the end of the second month, all cars had been positioned and on-time deliveries reached 85 percent. By the third month, the customer target was met. To this date, the business is the only supplier that has not put material on consignment at the customer, which provides a significant competitive advantage.

ENDNOTE

1. David Kiersey and Marilyn Bates, *Please Understand Me: Character and Temperament Types* (Del Mar: Prometheus Nemesis Book Co., 1984).

7

Ingredient 6: Rewards That Count

WHAT'S IN IT FOR ME?

All members of an organization are more interested in what they, as an individual, are realizing from their personal involvement with the organization than they are concerned about the overall performance of the business. Everyone! From the chairman on down, the question "What's in it for me?" rings loud and clear in the back of their minds. When the answer is "Not enough," people usually take one of three paths:

- They negotiate to get what they want.

- They quit and go somewhere else where they believe they will get what they want.

- They give up, make do with what they have, and stay where they are.

They quit working so hard, quit staying so late, and quit trying to make things happen.

Everyone works to satisfy his or her individual needs. Even people who devote their lives to charitable work do so to meet their own individual spiritual need. Therefore, any reward and recognition program must fundamentally satisfy the individual's desire, while driving the collective, collaborative behavior needed to optimize organizational performance.

THEORIES OF NEEDS

Abraham H. Maslow attempted to describe the intricacies of human behavior in his theory of the hierarchy of needs.[1] He defined the categories of needs as:

1. *Physiological needs*—the basic needs, such as the need for food, water, and sleep

2. *Safety needs*—the need for an ordered existence free from threats

3. *Love needs*—the need for affectionate relationships and the need to belong to groups

4. *Esteem needs*—the need for self respect, self esteem, and self satisfaction

5. *Self actualization needs*—the need for self fulfillment and achievement.

Maslow proposed that the needs are serially fulfilled. He believed that the behavior of any individual will be dominated by the lowest level of unfulfilled need.

Frederick Herzberg proposed a two-level need hierarchy: hygiene needs and motivator needs.[2] Hygiene needs include the lower-order needs described by Maslow and, in the workplace, such items as relative pay, security, general working conditions, rules, policies, and relationships with fellow workers. Motivator needs in the workplace include level of responsibility, freedom to perform independent action, and recognition of high performance.

Whichever theory of human behavior you believe, the major theme is that lower-level needs must be satisfied first. Only after the basic needs are satisfied will performance rewards be stimulating and motivating to the workforce.

This point seems to be missed in today's dog-eat-dog environment, in which Wall Street is continuously looking for next quarter earnings and many leadership teams are looking to reduce the workforce to boost earnings. Several companies repeatedly reduce staff year after year as a response to poor earnings, yet claim the reductions are planned productivity improvements designed to raise the company's fitness level. Some companies go too far and their actions do not result in a lean mean machine but rather a business with anorexia. These companies are lean but not fit. They are not capable of operating at the high performance levels required to compete in business today. Reducing staff to improve productivity destroys the companys' ability to perform. If your business is in this state, you need to get some stability and bring a sense of security to the minds of your workers.

In times of economic downturn, workforce reductions are sometimes inevitable. However, workforce reductions should be a last resort, well planned out, and designed to cause minimal disruption to the business. The onus is on the leadership team to spend its time developing a strategy that sustains profitability and growth and maintains a stable workplace.

T-SHIRTS AND HATS DON'T CUT IT!

I have seen many teams rewarded for their fine performance with a T-shirt, hat, or jacket, usually bearing the company logo. I'm sorry, but T-shirts and hats don't cut it! They should be given to recognize participation, not as a reward for a job well done. Rewards for a job well done should be substantial enough to motivate the recipient and observers to even higher levels of performance.

Most people go to work to support the lifestyle they want at home. In the early years of a career, people want to earn sufficient money to feed and clothe themselves and their families, and to put a roof over their heads. As time goes on, people want more—they want to buy a home, spend holidays abroad, drive newer and fancier cars, and have home computers, big-screen TVs, and the like. Later, they will want to invest in stocks and prepare for retirement.

As people's aspirations grow, so do their expectations. Human nature drives people to want what they see others around them have.

In this day and age, employees expect a fair day's pay for a fair day's work. Their perception of what's fair depends on several factors in the workplace. In my experience, people are pragmatic. I remember going to a mine in Arizona to see the work being done by a team of operators engaged in improving productivity in one of the subprocesses. They had implemented incredible productivity changes, and were all blue-collar workers. I asked many questions of the team members and they answered openly. So to reciprocate, I asked what did they want to know from me. A young lady stepped forward and said, "Hey, you're one of the vice presidents in this company. You get a fat salary and bonuses. What makes you think you're worth more than us?" I thought for a moment and responded, "I went to college for 12 years and worked hard to get three degrees. I have responsibility for 350 people, travel more than 90,000 miles a year, most often on my own time, and don't get to be with my family during the week like you do."

"Fair enough" she said and stepped back.

Most workers are realistic. They expect companies to be frugal in lean times, but they expect to be treated well in good years. Workers also expect to be treated with a certain level of equity and be rewarded for high performance.

Many people argue that nonmonetary rewards, such as workplace recognition, are motivational alternatives. I would argue that they are mandatory additions. If you do not have a reasonable work environment, treat people with respect and courtesy, and recognize their daily contributions, you do not deserve to have people working for you.

However, in my experience, substantial monetary rewards are by far the most effective for the majority of participants at any level of an organization. People respond to rewards (especially rewards they value highly) and will try to repeat the behavior they perceive they were rewarded for. Observers will also try to emulate the behavior that they believe is resulting in positive responses.

THE RECIPE'S EIGHT RULES FOR REWARD AND RECOGNITION

When you are building your reward and recognition system, take note of the following eight rules:

1. Rewards must be part of, and fit with, the overall compensation strategy of the organization.

2. Rewards and recognition must satisfy the basic needs first if higher-level rewards are to have the desired motivational effects.

3. Rewards and recognition must satisfy the individual's desire. In other words, rewards and recognition must be something that the individual values.

4. Rewards and recognition must drive the organizational need for collaborative work to optimize organizational performance.

5. Rewards and recognition must demonstrate equity across the whole company.

6. Expectations grow over time, so the reward mechanism should be growth oriented.

7. Rewards and recognition must be visible to the workforce so that its members can see what they have to do to get rewarded.

8. Without exception, no one should be rewarded for the wrong behavior.

Let's look at what has to be done to satisfy each rule.

Rule 1: Rewards Must Fit within the Overall Compensation Strategy

Just as each business improvement project has to fit within, and be related to, the strategic direction of the business, the rewards and recognition for the teams must fit within the overall compensation program of the company. Where many people fail is that they think of projects and their celebrations of successes as sort of "bolt-on goodies" that are attached to the business rather than being part of the everyday work of the organization. Part of the role of the senior leadership team is to ensure that the business improvement process gets folded into everyday life at the company. Only then can process improvement become part of the culture and second nature to the entire workforce. One of the major ways to do that is to make the compensation system supportive of the behavior that leaders want to establish. For example, CEO Jack Welch was reputed to be excellent at driving new behaviors into the culture at GE. He typically aligned the compensation programs—particularly promotions and bonuses for middle and senior managers—with the new processes he wanted to introduce.

The leadership team has to decide what behavior will get rewarded. Be consistent; if you want more teamwork across the organization, then set teaming as a goal for managers, and don't reward managers for being strong command-and-control characters who drive only for results. Each senior manager must sponsor at least one team, and learn at least the basic improvement techniques or no bonus and no promotion. People are boss-watchers and they will emulate the way their boss behaves. For this reason, concentrate first on getting the compensation program to mold the managers to the model you want. Then move on to the supervisors, again linking promotions, increases in job grading, and bonuses to the behavior you want. At lower levels of the organization, improvements in job grading can be linked to learning of the improvement techniques and involvement in successful teams.

Rule 2: Rewards and Recognition Must Satisfy the Basic Needs First

In 2000, the owners of a company announced they were going to sell the four subsidiaries that the company had diversified into and go back to just the core business. They began a process to try and sell the subsidiaries. Two years later, after the downturn of the economy, the owners announced they had changed their mind. They were going to keep and revive the noncore businesses. To this day, everyone remaining in the businesses does not believe them. After two years of no capital and waves of cutbacks in staffing and product lines, the owners' behavior still demonstrates intent to maximize returns to gain as favorable a sale as possible.

From the day of the first announcement, the employees have gathered at the coffee machines and photocopiers to discuss what's next. They struggle to maintain their focus on even the routine work, let alone work to raise performance. There is continuous turnover of those employees with a few years of service and the potential to go somewhere else. Many of the employees with long history of service have resigned themselves to wait it out to get the severance that they feel entitled to for all their past hard work. Even if the company does start to rebuild the noncore operations, it will be several years before the company has a truly motivated workforce once again.

All employees need a sense of safety and security at their place of work to turn in their best performance. I realize there are no guarantees in this life, but at least provide the best sense of security you can. The best way to do this is to have a clear strategy for winning the growth race, make that strategy well known to the workforce, and then, from the top down, commit to those actions that will make it happen. If you suffer a crisis that must result in a staff reduction, figure out what staffing you need and go to that level in one painful cut. Then reestablish your strategy, set about rebuilding the business, and start to rebuild the workers' confidence. Do not trim staffs in waves, quarter after quarter, letting a few go here and there. Such tactics will create a sense of insecurity in the workforce, and motivating them to achieve high performance will be a struggle.

The work environment is also important. Everyone desires meaningful work and a pleasant, stimulating work area. Most people respond well to managers who coach, involve, and persuade rather than those who command and control. Frequent use of simple forms of recognition are appreciated. The recognition can be verbal (simply saying "well done") or written (sending a thank-you note). Small gifts, such as a book, recognizing helpful and outstanding contributions can be given out frequently as people perform well. Allow people to make their work area pleasant and inviting so that their environment feels good to them. Although office space can sometimes be expensive, give as much as you can, and allow people the freedom to be comfortable in it.

Rule 3: Rewards and Recognition Must Satisfy the Individual's Desire

For a reward to be motivating, the receiver must personally perceive it as valuable. Team members are knowledgeable; they know that a hat is worth only a few dollars. For teams that generate substantial savings, a week's pay would be fair. If they're saving millions of dollars don't pay them peanuts! In addition, give a certificate or plaque spelling out why they received the reward, which they can proudly display in their work area or at home. If you give a certificate, frame it. Don't be a cheapskate. Be realistic. A starting reward should equate to a day's pay.

You can give employees a day off if you don't want to budget for rewards. Don't mess with gifts. Instead give gift certificates. A jacket, without the company logo, that a person can get some real use out of is just starting to enter into the realm of rewards.

Rule 4: Rewards and Recognition Must Satisfy the Organizational Need for Collaborative Work

At the end of the day, the objective of running improvement projects is to improve overall business performance. Whether the goal is profitability, growth in revenue, or something else, it's important that all functions recognize that the division or department goals are directly linked—and are subordinate to—the overall business goals.

The reward mechanism must drive collaboration so that if a particular project turns out to be absolutely critical, it will get the support needed from everyone. The strongest evidence of this collaboration is when a department manager gives up resources that will affect his or her own department goals for the greater good of the overall business. To create this collaborative atmosphere, the reward system must be flexible enough to recognize these sorts of sacrifices.

Basic common sense needs to be applied. If tracking of projects is ongoing, all managers will be well aware of resources being donated to greater causes. These resources that can be allowed for when assessing performance against goals.

Rule 5: Rewards and Recognition Must Demonstrate Equity across the Whole Company

Both the general compensation system and rewards and recognition system must be perceived as being reasonable and fair. Before employees will agree to commit, get involved, and strive for high performance, they must feel what they're getting is in line with what others are getting. This applies not just to colleagues working in similar jobs getting similar pay, but also to executives and all lower levels. For example, the workers will feel unfairly treated (and rightly so) if their wages are frozen because of an economic downturn but the executives are given tremendous stock packages. Any worker who feels unfairly treated will not give his or her best.

The reason why senior managers often fare best is that they are skilled negotiators. Rather than leave or sit back, they fight for what they want and often get it. At the other end of the chain, choosing to unionize is the way the general workforce gains leverage for negotiation.

Giving rewards that seem unequal can cause groups of people to become so annoyed that they resist future involvement. In one case, a maintenance supervisor led his team of mechanics to improve the shop's productivity by 50 percent. He was singled out for a chairman's award, and at a dinner ceremony, received a check for $5000. The following day, as he entered the shop, his workers turned their backs on him. Even though he intended to share the money with them, the damage was done. There was a core of team members who could not accept the unequal treatment the company had dished out. The workers got T-shirts while the supervisor received a significant monetary reward. The workers refused to further participate in the improvement process, and the team's performance slowly dwindled back to its old baseline.

One good way to reward the whole workforce is through gain-sharing. In this reward system, quarterly targets are set for the overall performance of the company or business unit. A formula is then applied that links meeting these quarterly targets to a payout for each individual. Quarterly payouts maintain the momentum to perform. Because all employees share in the gain, there's an incentive for workers to help or cover for others or to spend time on a team.

Rule 6: The Reward Mechanism Should Be Growth Oriented

In the current highly material world, almost everyone strives to get more. Particularly in the developed countries, what were once considered luxury items (color televisions, home computers) are now considered basics. Workers' expectations of what they consider reasonable earnings is driven by their perception of this ever increasing standard of living. However, just because they expect it, does not mean it's right to get it. Improvements in individual remuneration must be earned. In order to pay the workforce higher wages, any business must increase its profits while maintaining an adequate return to shareholders. In this context, *workforce* means everyone who makes their living out of the business—directors, managers, supervisors, and office and shop-floor workers.

Growth for the individual means performing at a higher level by working both harder and smarter. This improved productivity is reflected in compensation schemes through pay for performance (getting results) and pay for knowledge (the ability to bring smarter ways to work). Pay for knowledge is reflected in higher salary levels for positions that need higher levels of education, such as research scientists or strategic managers.

The bottom line, however, is the bottom line. Only by earning more can the organization pay more. This is why the results portion of the equation has to dominate, and why bonus payouts for all levels of the company must be linked to bottom-line growth.

Rule 7: Rewards and Recognition Must Be Visible So Everyone Understands What They Have to Do

In the same way that the strategic plan is openly communicated to the whole workforce, so should the compensation program and reward system be openly communicated. The compensation and reward system is designed to motivate people to perform to higher standards by working harder and smarter. One of the best motivational tools is to show them what they will attain if they are successful. I am not suggesting you open up the books and show what every employee earns to every other employee. What I am saying is that each individual has the right to know where he or she is on the compensation scale, why he or she is at that level, and what the person can do to enhance his or her position through improved performance, education and training, and so on. This approach empowers people to develop their own personal improvement plan.

The gain-sharing approach is particularly motivating when the payouts are explained in advance and the performance against the target is posted for all to see.

Promotions are one of the most visible events that occur in any organization. Be sure that when someone is promoted it is because they are demonstrating the performance and behaviors you are saying you want.

Rule 8: No One Should Be Rewarded for the Wrong Behavior

It's easy to reward the wrong behavior. One example I've seen is the manager who, noting that the president always went in to work on a Saturday, started visiting the office every Saturday morning. He rarely did any work, but made sure that the president saw him on every occasion. Sure enough, he got the next promotion and the workforce learned the lesson that attendance was more meaningful than hard work in that company.

In many companies, the style of workaholics is prized because they seem to be putting the company first. I have seen many workaholics during my career. A few are well organized and complete many tasks during their long days. They deserve their place high on the ladder because of their incredible hard work. Many others are workaholics because they are not good managers. They are poorly organized and inadequate at delegation. Hence, they struggle to complete their work in the allotted time. These people should not be praised for this inability but rather educated in how to manage their daily workload. All workaholics should be helped to bring balance to their life.

Promotions are a real test of a company's ability to see its stated intentions through. If you encourage teamwork but promote the "bully boy" that no one can stand, you send a strong message across the company that says the programs are BS. Similarly, if you want to encourage creativity but you always advance the people who toe the party line, do what they are told, and only follow the tried-and-tested traditional paths, you will stifle out-of-the-box thinking and build a legion of conformists.

In some cases, the wrong behavior needs to be dealt with severly and promptly. Bad behavior such as theft, fraud, and harassment in any form should not be tolerated. Get rid of any bad apples the moment you realize they are bad.

Human behavior is at best unpredictable. Following these eight rules will not guarantee success on all occasions, but they have been successfully used in other organizations.

I firmly believe that you should start with the premise that almost all people are honest and come to work wanting to do a good job. If you treat them with respect, you will build a firm foundation for empowerment and involvement. Furthermore, you should treat people in an open, equitable way and reward both good performance and the behavioral traits you want to develop. If you do so, you will build a team of winners, which is what every competitive organization needs.

ENDNOTES

1. Abraham H. Maslow, *Motivation and Personality* (New York: Harper and Row, 1970).
2. Frederick Herzberg, *Work and the Nature of Man* (New York: New American Library, 1978).

8

Making It Happen: The Journey of the Little Brick Company

STRATEGY FIRST

Arthur Gaylord was driving down the highway toward his new office on the outskirts of Birmingham. This was to be his first day as the managing director of the Little Brick Company (LBC). He landed this job because of his reputation for turning around other businesses that were struggling to perform. He had an uneasy feeling that this time it was going to be more difficult. He didn't even know the process for making bricks, and he knew even less about the markets being served.

He did know where he had to start the turnaround process, however. He knew that after meeting the staff, his first objective would be to better understand the business so he could clarify the company's strategic direction. He once heard someone say, "People who don't know where they are going usually end up somewhere else." He was firmly convinced that, for success, the first order of business was to clearly establish where he wanted LBC to head over the next five years.

It was only 7 AM when he stepped through the front door. He could hear raised voices from a conference room at the end of the hall. He ventured down to see what was going on, and as he pushed the door open, the room went silent. He introduced himself to the three people inside. They were Keith Shock, the plant manager, Mary Evans, the sales manager, and Don Forth, the person in charge of warehousing and transport.

"Boy am I glad to see you," said Mary. "We had a disaster last night, and we're going to have to choose which of several customers don't get their bricks this week."

Keith went on to explain that the large industrial complex next to the brick plant had a boiler failure in the night, and a plume of thick black smoke had contaminated almost a quarter of the good bricks at the south end of the site. These bricks could not be sent to any customers. It would take three product changes on the line to make all the bricks needed and that would create a pile of scrap that the company could not afford. Don wanted approval to throw the contaminated bricks in the local refuse dump so he had space to put the replacements.

Arthur knew he must not be drawn so early into the quagmire of day-to-day operations, but he saw the opportunity to expose these three managers to some of his key management beliefs.

"Mary, be open and tell all of the customers about the problem. Ask for their cooperation in taking only what they absolutely need while we get operations back on track. Ken, make the production changes needed to keep our customers as happy as possible. Don, let's not do anything with the contaminated bricks until we have a clear understanding of the facts. Maybe they can be cleaned." Arthur left them to handle the crisis and went off to find his office.

He sat down to plan out the rest of the day, which would be spent becoming acquainted with the staff, touring the manufacturing process, and starting to understand the business.

By the end of the week, Arthur was feeling good about his progress. He had read the last three annual reports, looked at the last two years of monthly updates, and talked at length to every manager on site about the business.

The plant was designed and built five years ago by John Little, a local entrepreneur who owned the land and discovered fine alluvial clay on the site, which is perfect for making bricks. A brick-making machine had been imported from Korea because it was only half the cost of locally offered equipment. The plant was designed to make 30 million bricks a year, but output had never exceeded 22 million. The market had proven much tougher than expected, and the original plan to gain five percent market share had never come to fruition. Worse still, with a poor quality reputation, LBC had no leverage on pricing. Over the five years LBC had been in business, it made money only once and broke even for the other four years.

Arthur was now ready to set up the first strategic review with his leadership team. He called them all together to decide the best place to hold the session. He told them that it would be an off-site meeting in which he could be sure of their complete attention, without interruption. They reached the consensus to hold the meeting on the following weekend in private conference rooms at a local hotel. Arthur asked them to be prepared for long days and to bring along as much information as possible about the business, particularly customers and competitors.

At 8 AM on Saturday, Arthur opened the session by asking the group, "What business are we in?"

The unanimous response was, "The brick business."

A discussion ensued about how the clay would also be good for making dinnerware. However, because this operation would require a highly skilled labor force and a complete change of equipment, it was not a feasible alternative.

Arthur's second question was, "How are we currently trying to compete?"

Mary jumped in and responded "We have no choice. The market demands high-quality products at low cost. Every time I go to a customer, I'm told that the Large Brick Company's product is much more uniform than ours and its prices are lower. We have to be the low-cost producer."

"As I've told you before," Ken retorted, "that company uses the latest extrusion machines, which run at very close tolerance and put out three times more bricks than our machine in a day. We can't expect to match that unless we buy new machines."

After considerable discussion, the group agreed the approach they were following was to try to serve all customers as well as they could. Next Arthur asked, "Who are our customers and what do they want?"

Mary shared an extensive market report with the whole group. The total number of bricks used this year would be 600 million, with LBC supplying 20 million or 3.3 percent. The Large Brick Company would supply 90 percent of the market needs, and the remainder would be imported. Two major markets existed for bricks: new homes and old homes being refurbished. The large home builders predominantly bought from the Large Brick Company because they wanted to build homes quickly and the bricks' uniformity gave them fewer problems and a need for less-skilled bricklayers. LBC was favored by the small builders because the less uniform bricks gave an upscale appearance to the finished homes. LBC enjoyed much higher pricing with these small builders, but was losing money supplying to the new-home market overall because of the large discounts demanded by the professional teams of buyers at the large builders.

When questioned about other potential markets, Mary said she had looked at the prospect of having the bricks used in office buildings, which were predominantly concrete. She conceded after talking with a few customers, who said they did not want the mess of dealing with brick.

Arthur led two brainstorm sessions on the strengths and weaknesses of LBC and its competitors. With this information, he created the comparison chart that Table 8.1 shows.

As the group reviewed the chart, it became obvious that there was no way LBC could compete on cost with the other suppliers. They would have to develop a strategy to take a larger portion of the small builder market. In that arena, LBC seemed to be better satisfying customers' needs and was able to sustain higher pricing. They discussed this strategy over dinner that

Table 8.1   Comparison of LBC and its competitors.

LBC	Large Brick Company	Imports
Strengths		
Aesthetic look once built into a wall	Uniformity in bricks' shape, size, and color	Very low cost from Asian sources
Variation in color looks better in finished building	High-throughput machines give low cost	
Flexibility—willing to supply small lots	Larger production capability favored by large customers	
Weaknesses		
High production cost	Less flexible—will only supply full truck lots	Delivery unreliable
No capital available for investment	Bloom problem—bricks get white crystals on surface while weathering	No customer support if needed

night. The old strategy was "trying to supply bricks at any cost to whoever wanted them." They felt happy about what was starting to come into focus as the new strategy: "Being the premier supplier to the small builders market, by offering tailored products and services to their chosen customers."

As a sales manager, Mary felt good about this approach. The sales representatives were continually complaining about how much they hated dealing with the buyers at the major builders, who beat them up over price every time they visited. It would be a pleasure to direct the sales group to spend more time with the smaller companies. As the plant manager, Ken was more nervous. Product changeovers took two days and caused large amounts of scrap, and he knew the sales force would soon be asking for a slew of new products.

Tim Fry, the chief accountant, did a quick calculation on his napkin at the dinner table. He let everyone know that based on the current pricing, for every million bricks switched from large to small customers, they would improve profits by $100,000.

Arthur knew that it would take action across all functions of the business if they were to grow the small builders' market share. Besides, he wasn't so happy to simply exchange share. He wanted to grow to the 30 million brick output that was originally planned for the business.

On the morning of the second day, Arthur exposed his idea to the group. He agreed that growth should concentrate on the small builder market, but also felt that by improving operations, they should be able to attain competitiveness and stay at the current level in the large builder market. They would have to find new ways to serve that market rather than walk away from it. He revealed his 30 million brick output target, and everyone thought it was a great idea, except Ken, who said it would be impossible unless he was allowed to change all the equipment.

The rest of the day they debated about and reached consensus on the vision and key goals for the business. Ken bought into the consensus when Arthur told him that he would like to explore every other possible method for improving output first, but as a last resort, he would agree to replace equipment if the other methods failed.

The group members documented the vision as:

Little Brick Company will grow by being the premier supplier to the builders market by offering tailored products and services to our chosen customers.

They set the targets for that growth as:

Key Measures	Now	Target
Sales revenue	$5 million	$8 million
Market share	3.3%	5%
Profitability	$0	$1.5 million

They also agreed that the timetable was to reach this point in 3 years and that in the first year their key milestone was to be showing at least $200,000 improvement on the bottom line. That way, the directors would have faith that they were capable of turning the company around.

Arthur was pleased with the enthusiasm shown by the leadership team. He now wanted to start the involvement of the next level of managers, gain their buy-in, and gather their ideas for how to move forward. There were a total of 225 people employed at LBC. He asked each member of the leadership team to present him with a list of managers and supervisors that should be in the next session. He wanted every function to be represented, and at least five people from each of the major areas of sales, manufacturing, technical, finance, and shipping. He knew that if the top 10 percent of the people in the company became enthusiastically involved, they would be the force needed to drive the whole organization to its goals. He also wanted to move quickly and have the strategic direction set within a month.

The next session was set up for two days in the same off-site conference center, but this time it would be during the week. Arthur wanted to make the point that this was so important that all key managers must attend. By holding it on normal workdays, no personal excuse for lack of attendance could be offered. It was also a chance to establish that daily operations could go on for at least a few days without the constant attention of management.

In the opening session, Arthur and the leadership team started by sharing all of the information they had used in their own session and went on to describe how they had come to their vision and goals for the organization. They opened the floor to discussion before asking the group for its commitment to the vision and goals.

Next, Arthur split the group members into their natural work functions—five teams in all. Arthur asked each team to develop the mission and goals for its work area, which would support the overall mission and business objectives. The five teams worked on their mission and goals the rest of the day.

On day two, Arthur started the morning by reminding the five teams about the vision and goals for the overall business. He pointed out that the mission for each function should be aligned and supportive of them. The teams then proceeded to report on the mission and goals for their work areas. At the end of the day, after feedback and debate, the mission and goals for the five functions were:

Sales

Mission: Sell more bricks.

Objectives:

1. Grow sales from 20 to 30 million units.

2. Grow sales with small builders from 10 to 20 million units.

3. Maintain sales at large builders at 10 million units.

Manufacturing

Mission: Make bricks needed by customers with better quality at lower cost.

Objectives:

1. Increase throughput from 20 to 30 million units.

2. Reduce production cost from 0.25 cents to 0.225 cents per unit.

3. Improve quality of bricks (first step—size uniformity).

Supply and Shipping

Mission: Make sure all materials and finished goods are delivered on time at lowest cost.

Objectives:

1. Reduce cost of materials by 5 percent.

2. Improve on-time delivery rate to 95 percent.

Technical

Mission: Develop new products identified by sales.

Objectives:

1. Extend product range for small builders.

2. Develop handmade substitutes that command high price.

Finance and Administration:

Mission: Improve reporting and communication processes.

Objectives:

1. Improve reporting so that operating managers can make better decisions.

2. Issue monthly communications to whole workforce to keep everyone up to speed with programs.

3. Find ways to reduce processing to make it easier for customers to do business with LBC.

In some areas, the goals were not yet specific enough for Arthur. He liked to have measurements and milestones in place for each. However, he was satisfied that they were good enough to go to the next level and start the detailed business diagnostics to find the meaningful areas in which projects could be found.

BUSINESS DIAGNOSTICS

Arthur decided to perform the business diagnostics in two steps. First, he'd create a macro review of the overall business with the leadership team.

Then, he'd create a more detailed dig down into each functional area with the process managers for each department.

The macro review with the leadership team was another daylong affair. The agenda for the day was:

- *Session 1*—What is happening in the marketplace?

  – With customers

  – With competitors

- *Session 2*—What is happening with the money?

  – Review profit and loss, balance sheet, and cost center reports.

  – What is our cost of quality?

- *Session 3*—What is happening within each major function?

  – What are the key performance indicators for each process?

  – How well are the processes performing?

- *Session 4*—How is time being spent?

  – What are the cycle times for key processes?

  – What percent of time is value-added?

- *Session 5*—What ideas does the team have?

  – Other areas that need investigation.

All of the leadership team members admitted they had never been through such a review before and that looking at all of the areas of the business together gave them a better understanding of the issues each had been facing. They also quickly pinpointed some areas that warranted further research:

- In the sales area, they discovered that the largest cause of lost sales for small customers was unavailability of bricks.

- In the cost review, they noted that sand, while being less than five percent of the unit by weight, was responsible for 28 percent of the unit cost.

- In the manufacturing area, the machine was actually producing at the rate of over 27 million units but 18 percent were being lost in the next step (the drying process) because they cracked.

Each leadership team member was now charged with holding a similar review within their functions. Arthur insisted that they lead the next reviews themselves. If they needed his help, he would help them prepare and set their agenda, but it was time for them to step forward and lead the process. Arthur would attend the ending session of each review to discuss the findings.

Mary brought all of her salespeople into the plant for their meeting. She felt it was a wonderful opportunity for them to get to see the manufacturing process, which many of them had never done. The diagnostic focused on better understanding the market, customers, and competitors. Mary asked the questions:

- Do we know what our customers want?

- What are the reasons we lose sales to competitors?

- In what markets or niches do we have competitive advantage and why?

- Where do competitors do better than us and why?

The session was very eye-opening. John, who was key account manager for many of the larger builders, said, "We wouldn't have any problems with these customers if we would just sort the bricks to give a blend of colors on a pallet like we used to do. The larger builders refuse to select bricks from several pallets like the smaller builders do. They want to just use the bricks as they arrive."

All of the people who sold to the small builders agreed they could sell much more if only the delivery time could be guaranteed. "We keep promising two weeks and then miss, so they go buy Large Brick Company bricks off the shelf. They love our bricks, and they charge premiums for the homes built with them. But they can't stop their building process because we don't deliver on time," said Fred.

The sales group also noted that it could sell many more of the standard products if the plant would produce just a few special shapes that the builders could use to enhance the appearance of corners and gables. Price was not considered an issue by the group, even for the large customers. Mary summed it up "We are always on the defensive because of supply and blending issues and our only response is to reduce the price."

Ken's session with the manufacturing managers and supervisors was held the following day. He asked Tim Fry to help him present the financial data and stay all day to help with any number crunching.

The numbers showed that the major cause of the high costs was indeed the 18 percent scrap that was coming out of the dryer. The manufacturing team had never really concerned themselves with this scrap because the material was immediately ground up and put back in the mixer of the machine. So, they never considered they lost anything. The problem was the machine was making close to 27 million bricks a year, but they were only getting at best 22 million out to customers. If they could prevent just half of this loss, they could add $250,000 to the bottom line.

The second area recognized as a major cause of customer quality issues was control in the firing process. Underheating caused oversized bricks; overheating caused undersized bricks.

Tim Fry also attended Don's session with the shipping group to ensure those team members had a good understanding of the financial levers. The waste in this area was not so clear. There were some pointers that the order entry and delivery promise system was broken, but it was not clear what the problems were. Don was also responsible for purchasing and was surprised at the high cost of sand, but pointed out that LBC had always used the same source since the business opened. The supplier was a friend of Mr. Little.

The diagnostics continued across the whole business, until each member of the leadership team and their managers had a pretty good understanding of the areas they needed to improve. Arthur was pleased. He was now six weeks into the improvement process and they were ready to select the projects. He called another leadership team meeting. He wanted to be sure the team stayed focused. Each leadership team member was told to bring every form and report that was issued in their department to the conference room, prior to the start of the meeting.

BASIC TRAINING

The meeting day had arrived and everyone was assembled in the conference room. Arthur began the meeting by explaining what the STOP process was and how he personally had completed it once every three months for the last two years in his last place of employment. Everyone in LBC was going to learn how to use this process, and he was going to start right now by getting the team to decide which of the reports they brought were adding value. Those reports that didn't add value were going to be eliminated.

After two hours, the team had divided the pile of papers on the conference room table into a keep stack and toss stack. They decided they would check with the rest of the organization before they junked the toss pile just to be sure they weren't breaking any laws or making any big mistakes. (Within a week, almost all of the papers in the toss pile were gone. Total reporting had been cut by a third.)

The leadership team spent the afternoon reviewing their roles and responsibilities. They agreed to use the STOP process across the board to cut wasteful activity.

There was no one within the business, other than Arthur, who had been exposed to the statistical tools and problem-solving methods that would be needed to fix the identified problems. The group decided to use an outside resource to provide the needed training. The local technical college provided two lecturers well versed in the tools and techniques of quality management. They met with Arthur to finalize the training outline and review the 90-day project methodology he wanted to use.

Just two weeks later, the leadership team members attended the first training class, which taught them how to use the seven simple statistical tools and the five problem-solving techniques. They wanted to both understand the tools and techniques and demonstrate to the rest of the workforce how committed they were to the program, so they each agreed to sponsor teams in their areas. Arthur gave them copies of his crib sheet "10 Steps to Managing Teams" to help them through the process.

Training for other teams would be conducted after the projects and teams were chosen. But before that, Arthur wanted to be sure the whole workforce understood what was going on. He wanted every employee to have a clear understanding of the vision, missions, and goals for each department. He also wanted every employee to know that issues would be solved by project teams using a consistent approach.

Tim put together the package and prepared some transparencies that could be used to make the presentation. The whole leadership team agreed to present the material and set up four sessions, including one at 8 PM for the night shift. This session was a real surprise to that group because they had always been made to stay past their shift to attend information or training sessions in the morning. This was the first time that management had scheduled a meeting during their shift. Some workers wondered whether it signaled a layoff or closure because they knew the plant was not profitable. They were quite relieved when the presentation ended. In the question-and-answer session that followed, Ken was amazed by their flow of ideas on how to improve operations. He had never seen the group so charged up.

PROJECTS THAT GET RESULTS

Ken came to see Arthur the following morning. The diagnostic in manufacturing had identified 10 or more areas in which action could be taken. Because of the enthusiastic response and the many ideas from the shift workers, he wanted to strike while the iron was hot. Ken proposed a dozen teams to start attacking the waste in the manufacturing area. Arthur reminded him about the Pareto principle and suggested that he identify the few projects that would have the largest impact. Arthur also reminded Ken that some of the key projects in other areas might need the manufacturing group's help, so he should leave some resources available for that.

"I only want to start 10 projects in total across the whole business," said Arthur at the following leadership meeting. "If we have just five people on each team, that's 50 in total, almost a quarter of the workforce. We need to focus on the major issues in the first wave. This group has to decide today what those projects will be."

Tim suggested they start by agreeing on the criteria that any project would have to meet before being considered. After some debate and discussion, they had a sheet of flipchart paper pinned up on the wall. On it was written:

Selection criteria for projects:

- Must fit with strategic direction.

    - Growth with small customers and maintaining large customers through targeted offerings

- Must better satisfy customers' needs.

    - Better products, improved quality, and lower cost

- Must improve performance this year.

    - With need to show positive performance, must increase revenue or reduce cost in relatively short period of time

Ken commented that he had several projects that met the criteria, but realized he should start only two or three to maintain focus. He explained how he had already done a Pareto analysis, which showed that three projects account for 55 percent of the potential profit improvements the business needs. He suggested that they each prioritize projects within their area and offer four or five for consideration prior to a vote on which were most important for the company overall.

By lunch time they had the list of 10 projects:

1. Reduce scrap from brick dryer.

2. Improve dimension control of bricks in the kiln.

3. Reduce changeover time for brick type (currently two days).

4. Increase share of southern region small builders by one million bricks.

5. Make special shapes available in order to win Border Builder contract for two million bricks.

6. Find alternative sand sources in order to reduce cost of raw material.

7. Improve scheduling and quoting process so delivery can be guaranteed for small builders.

8. Find a way to blend bricks to satisfy large customers' needs.

9. Improve inventory control to reduce cash tied up in excess stock.

10. Develop method for making replacements for 100-year-old bricks that currently are supplied from demolished buildings and sell at 10 times standard brick price.

Project 10 has a longer time frame. However, it was included because the group felt it should not completely abandon all long-term projects.

The leadership team members took on their role as sponsors for the projects. Ken would sponsor projects 1, 2, and 3. Mary had projects 4 and 5. Don agreed to take projects 6 and 8, but was worried that he had little understanding of the computer programs involved with project 7. Tim agreed to sponsor that one along with project 9. The final project, number 10, would be sponsored by Joe Johnson, the technical manager who reported to Ken.

The 10 teams had their kickoff sessions the mornings and afternoons of the following week. The sponsor started each four-hour session by going over the team charter for the project and giving the team members permission to identify waste that could be cut out to make things easier. Then the team went into their first team meeting, during which one of the trainers explained the process-mapping methodology and had them start to map the target process. Meetings were held each week with a trainer, who took the first hour to teach a new tool or technique. There were times when a trainer wasn't available, but the teams got by. In some cases, they just learned about the tool or technique from the materials they had been given.

After the teams had been running for a month, Arthur set aside two days to have the sponsors and leaders report on how the projects were going. Tim asked him to let the whole team come into the session because he felt that the workforce was beginning to appreciate the more open communication.

Each team's feedback session was a learning experience for Arthur. As he reviewed the process maps and the rest of the data being analyzed, his worries about not understanding the brick-making process were dispelled.

The manufacturing teams had confirmed that cracks were occurring across the middle of some bricks while the bricks were in the dryer. They were now linking a computer to one dryer to check whether the rate of temperature increase was the cause. They had also identified that kiln temperature control was once good, but had gone bad when the instrument calibration service was cut to save maintenance expense. They were reinstituting the service and would monitor performance. The changeover team had identified a product change sequence that would reduce cycle losses by almost 50 percent. The team was starting to coordinate its work with the scheduling team.

The sales projects were going well also. One team had identified that in the southern region, sales representatives had neglected to spend time with the small builders. The sales representatives had now been visiting them and the orders were already flowing in. Manufacturing had set up an operation to make the special shapes needed for Border Builders and a quote for the business was under review by Border's senior buyer.

The purchasing team had found three alternate sources for sand, which were now under test. The team also started discussions with the current supplier about how costs could be reduced.

The blending team had met only twice and was still struggling to put the initial process map together. Arthur asked what help it needed to be able to get the project back on track. The team was made up of shipping staff members and as the small orders were increasing, they were struggling to find the time. Don agreed to look at how to make the time available.

On the inventory front, the contaminated bricks from the boiler incident were the biggest concern. They were held on the books at a value of $200,000, which Tim did not want to write off unless absolutely necessary. Otherwise, the team had already started to put in place administrative measures that would free up almost $300,000 in cash flow by the end of the year.

Joe Johnson detailed how his team had visited refurbishing companies that used bricks salvaged from demolished buildings to repair other old buildings. The key criterion was to have a brick that was aged with a hundred years of smoke and grime. The team was experimenting with different dyes to try to mimic that effect.

Arthur felt pleased at the end of the two-day review. Nine of the teams had reported eagerly on their progress. Only the blending team appeared to be struggling to make headway, and Don had committed to fulfill his sponsor role and help the team find its way back on track.

Some of the teams appeared to be finding breakthrough solutions already, and the prospects of winning the Border business—an extra sale of two million bricks—looked excellent. The path forward was beginning to look a little easier to tread.

Mary had been asking Arthur to set aside time to visit some of the major customers with her. He told her to schedule some appointments over the next two weeks. He suggested that one of the visits be with Border. Maybe that company could help the projects along.

Two weeks later, Arthur and Mary sat down to dinner with John Border, president of Border Builders. This was the first time Mary managed to convince John to have dinner, and she knew it was Arthur's presence that tempted him to come. Over dinner, John questioned Arthur at length about the approach he was taking to turn around LBC. He showed genuine interest and was particularly attentive when Arthur explained his approach of focusing on a few key projects that could be successfully concluded in a relatively short period of time.

"That's certainly an approach to try at Border," said John. "We are always overpromising and underdelivering because we stretch ourselves too thin."

Mary saw the opportunity to ask about the prospects for the tender and was shocked when John responded, "It's a very good tender, but I am reluctant to give you the business this time around because of your terrible delivery performance in the past. We need to see evidence that you have overcome your delivery problems to the industry. I would think there's every chance you could get the business next year."

On the journey back, Arthur and Mary figured out they had just 60 days to convince John that LBC had in place a robust ordering and delivery system. Ensuring on-time delivery was now the critical factor if the Border business was to come to LBC.

On returning to the plant, Arthur and Mary met with the rest of the leadership team and gave feedback from all of their visits. The two large builders they had visited were adamant that the cost of doing business was all they were interested in. All of the small builders they visited told them that the product was great, but delivery performance must improve.

Arthur asked Tim Fry, sponsor of the scheduling team, to share the small builders' and John's feedback with that team. The team was meeting the following day, and Tim dropped in to give the feedback. The team responded, saying that it could put a process in place immediately that would ensure Border deliveries if Border could give four weeks' notice of requirements instead of the customary two. Mary was called in and the group informed her of how it might be done. Mary agreed to call the buyer and see if he was amenable to a four-week order notice. Mary returned to the meeting with a big smile on her face. The buyer could actually give six weeks' notice because that was Border's standard scheduling period.

At the 60-day review, Mary asked if the shapes team could present first because of the importance of this project. Arthur reminded the leadership team, "All 10 projects are critical to our future. Let's give every team the attention it deserves."

The manufacturing group started. The dryer team had reached an impasse and needed the leadership team's direction to move forward. The team members could follow two routes. The computer trials indicated that they could reduce the cracking by 50 percent if they had precise control over the steam flow. Modifying all the dryers would cost $300,000 and the engineers in the group wanted to modify the first dryer at a cost of $30,000. However, the operators on the team said they felt the problem initiated in the brick-making machine because the press no longer squashed the water out like it did in the first few months of operation. Because of maintenance problems at that time, the cam was changed to reduce the pressure. Operators were convinced the $30,000 should be spent on a machine rebuild and cam upgrade.

The leadership team listened intently and, after considerable discussion, told the dryer team to go ahead with the machine rebuild. Ken indicated that the rebuild would be necessary in the next year anyway; if it solved the cracking problem, then the money to computerize the dryer would be saved.

Next, the kiln team gave its report. The team members reported that by putting instrument calibration service back in place on the kiln, the number of wrong-sized bricks had been reduced by 40 percent. They were now putting together new Pareto charts to decide which cause to tackle next.

The changeover and scheduling teams reported that they had implemented the new product sequence. As a result, changeovers were now creating one-third less scrap. The teams also reported that they planned to implement a stock-replenishment program to handle the projected Border business. If this program proved successful, it would be extended across the whole business.

In anticipation of the new Border contract, the shapes team had streamlined the process for making the special-shaped bricks. The team members assured everyone that they could meet the schedule with no problem.

In the purchasing area, two of the new sands tested turned out to be darker red than the existing sand and could not be used as replacements. However, the existing sand supplier had dropped its price by 10 percent because it was concerned that it might lose all or a portion of LBC's business. In addition, Joe Johnson said that R&D was now looking at the darker-red sand because several customers had requested bricks in darker colors.

The inventory team reported that the inventory controls it put in place were having an effect. No products were being scheduled for manufacture if there was more than three weeks' stock. The team also reported that it was reconfiguring the layout of the warehouse so that similar products are together and more easily located. Due to its involvement in this activity, the blending team said that it met only once and made no progress on its own project.

In response to the blending team's report, Arthur made the point that, by neglecting this project, the group was putting the large-customer business at risk. "Large customers want hassle-free, low-cost products and services from us," said Arthur. "It is essential this team develop a blending process to meet those needs." Arthur then made a mental note to himself to immediately become involved in coaching Don and this team. He chastised himself for not having done so after the 30-day review.

Finally, Joe reported on the long-term project to develop replacements for very old bricks. The team members had found two water-soluble dyes that would age bricks. The method of application was to spray the dyed water over pallets of bricks. Joe noted that they were taking great care not to contaminate any of the drainage water systems and that they were using the smoke contaminated bricks for the trials.

Two days later Arthur had a meeting with Don to find out why the blending team was not moving forward with its project. He asked for the team charter and Don admitted he had never prepared one for this team. "They have all been involved in blending in the past. They know what to do, restart manual blending like we did a year ago," said Don.

"It's not a question of restarting what we did before," responded Arthur. "Every team must be given a clear problem and permitted to solve it. Don, you have just given them your solution to implement, and that is not acceptable. The methodology must be followed. Let's go back to square one. We'll prepare a team charter, bring the team together, and restart the project."

Don and Arthur put together the team charter, which Figure 8.1 shows. They then called the team together.

The team members were nervous at first. However, after Arthur explained that he was not looking to blame anyone for the slow progress, merely help Don to bring the team back on track, they relaxed and opened up. The whole group was unhappy with going back to the old system. It was very labor-intensive and they felt it did not reduce the number of complaints that large brick companies made. They wanted the opportunity to explore new options but were limited in the time being allowed for them to work together on the project.

Don agreed to run a STOP process with them. Arthur authorized overtime for the team members so that they could meet twice a week instead of the usual once per week to catch up.

The team members set off with renewed vigor and even met once on their own time at Susan's house on a Saturday morning. Things were back on track.

Project title	Blending project
Sponsor	Don Forth
Leader	Susan
Members	Tom, Dick, Mary, and Bert
Project goal	Establish new blending process to ensure bricks supplied to large customers meet their needs.
Deliverables	New process that takes bricks from kiln and blends them to the uniformity standard required by large customers.
Key performance measures	Uniformity of bricks on pallets prepared for large customers. Reduced rejections by large customers for poor uniformity.
Boundaries	Capital spending needs managing director's approval. Changes in kiln emptying operation must be agreed with manufacturing. Changes in staffing roles need department manager's approval.
Critical dates	Start date: past 30-day review: past 60-day review: 3/5 Target finish date: 4/5

Figure 8.1 Blending team charter.

START CELEBRATING

Ken burst into Arthur's office. "Come on, you're invited for a celebration pizza with the manufacturing group. The rebuilt machine has been back online for two days and dryer scrap is running at less than two percent!"

As they walked into the plant, Ken explained that the pizza was being provided by the two engineers on the team. They had lost a bet with the operators that modifying the machine would have no effect. The happy atmosphere in the plant canteen as the operators enjoyed their moment of glory was uplifting for all. Arthur thought that maybe a barbecue after the 90-day report would be a good way to have the whole workforce join the celebrations.

There were still 10 days to go before that magic date when all of the projects were due. Only the blending project would not be complete. Arthur coached Don and the team back into the routine of following the methodology, but with the time lost during the first 60 days, they would need another month to finish. They were now meeting twice a week and potential solutions looked very promising. Arthur blamed only himself for taking his eye off the ball and not stepping up the coaching activity earlier.

All of the other projects would be completed on time, and the results were astonishing. The cracked brick issue was solved and the number of wrong-sized bricks was cut in half. These improvements, coupled with the reduced price of sand, brought the cost down to $0.23 per unit. Sales in the South were on target, and Border was giving them one third of its business this year. The increased throughput, due to reduced scrap, was resulting in better availability for small builders and sales were growing dramatically. Improved inventory control and scheduling was also impacting on-time delivery, which looked likely to set a record of 90 percent this month.

At the next weekly leadership meeting, Tim Fry reviewed the financial projections. If current performance levels held, LBC would finish the year with revenue of $6 million from sales of 24 million units. He predicted profits would be approximately $450,000. It was time to truly celebrate, and Arthur wanted the leadership team to plan the celebration.

The barbecue was held on the front lawn of the office complex. It was held there so that the working shift could at least come up in groups and participate. In the conference room, tables were set up displaying the project reports and photographs of the team members.

Arthur opened the event by bringing each team up to the front, making a few comments about their success, and awarding each member a plaque and a $50 gift certificate. He pointed out to the group that the only group not receiving an award that day was the blending team members because they had not finished their project. He expected they would be there in 30 more days and that would be an excuse for at least a pizza lunch.

Before allowing everyone to eat, Arthur had one further message for the assembly. He had just received approval from the board of directors to pay a one-week bonus at the end of the year to all employees if the target of $400,000 profitability was met.

"In that case," shouted a voice from the back, "we better forget the food and start the next 10 projects!"

Arthur laughed along with everyone else, but he knew it was true. The next wave of projects needed to be started soon. As he joined the line for food, he thought back over his time at LBC. During the first month, he developed the strategic direction with the top two levels of the organization. The second month was spent on two weeks of diagnostics, followed by the start of basic training. The first wave of focused projects was launched in the third month. The fourth and fifth months gave rise to the 30-day and 60-day reviews of the teams' progress. The current month was filled with the teams' final reports and this joyous celebration. He felt comfortable that this business turnaround was successfully under way.

Appendix A

90-Day Project Methodology Timetable

Phase	Step	Tools to use	Time to complete
Project setup	Kickoff meeting	Project selection worksheet Team charter STOP process worksheets	4 hours
Understanding	1. Define process 2. Map process (macro view) 3. Map process (micro view)	Process definition worksheet Process mapping	2 weeks
Analysis	4. Analyze process	Seven simple statistical tools	2 weeks
30-day review			
	4. Further analysis	Seven simple statistical tools	1 week
Potential solutions	5. Brainstorm improvements	Problem-solving tools Trials and experiments	3 weeks
60-day review			
Implement improvements	6. Map new process	Process mapping Action lists	2 weeks
Sustain improvements	7. Control new process	Procedures documented Training completed Control measures in place	2 weeks
90-day review			

Appendix B

90-Day Project Methodology Worksheets

90-Day Project Methodology Worksheet 1	
Step 1: Define the process	
Name of the process:	
Purpose:	
Outputs: • Products • Services • By-products	
Customers:	
Inputs:	
Boundaries:	
Value added:	

90-day Methodology Worksheet 2	
Step 2: Map the process (macro view)	
Identify the critical activities	
Define the sequence of activities	
Draw as simple a picture as possible to represent the process	Put this on a flipchart
Have everyone review the map and modify until agreement reached	
Step 3: Map the process (micro view)	
Add in the major subprocesses • What • When • Where • Who • How • How long	Add this to the flipchart
Ask the five whys	
Note details on the process map	When Who ACTIVITY What Where Time
Have everyone review the map and modify until agreement reached	

90-Day Project Methodology Worksheet 3	
Step 4: Analyze the process	
Key performance indicator Customer satisfaction levels	
Key performance indicator Partner and supplier satisfaction levels	
Key performance indicator Cycle times Delays Costs	
Key performance indicator Waste Variation	
Gather data to understand how process is performing Use the seven simple statistical tools	
Analyze data to identify problem areas	
Prepare graphs and charts that show a picture of performance	
Evaluate competitor approaches	
Benchmark noncompetitive processes	

90-Day Project Methodology Worksheet 4	
Step 5: Brainstorm improvements	For each activity
Purpose: What added value does this activity provide? What is actually done or achieved? Why is this activity necessary? What else might be done?	
Place: Where is it being done? Why is it done there? Where else might it be done?	
Sequence: When is it being done? Why is it done then? When might it be done?	
Method: How is it done? Why is it done that way? How else might it be done?	
Which problems recur? Which errors occur? How might technology help?	

90-Day Project Methodology Worksheet 5	
Step 6: Map the new process	
Identify the critical activities	
Define the new sequence	
Define the new information flow	
Identify subprocesses and their sequence	
Draw the macro and micro maps of the new process	
Obtain buy-in from all parties	
Implement the changes	
Step 7: Control the new process	
Document new procedures	
Ensure everyone is trained	
Ensure control measures are in place	
Implement feedback and control—is the process meeting key performance indicator targets?	
Complete project report	
Celebrate!	Look for the next improvement project

Appendix C
Process Definition Worksheet

Process Definition Worksheet

Process name:

Purpose:

Inputs	Core activities	Outputs
1.	1.	1.
2.	2.	2.
3.	3.	3.
4.	4.	4.
5.	5.	5.
6.	6.	6.

Suppliers	Improvement objective	Customers
A.		A.
B.		B.
C.		C.

Sponsor: Team: Leader:

Appendix D

Cascading Goals Worksheet

Cascading Goals Worksheet	
Vision for the business:	Key performance measures: 1. 2. 3. 4. 5.
Mission for department:	Key goals: 1. 2. 3.

How do these relate to the vision and mission?	Key activities 1. 2. 3. 4. 5. 6.	*How will they help attainment of the goals?*

Questions:

A. Does the mission of the department support the vision of the business? How?

B. Do the goals of the department support the key performance measures? How?

C. Are the key activities in line with the vision, mission, and goals? How?

Appendix E
Project Selection Worksheet

Project Selection Worksheet	
Mission for department:	Key goals: 1. 2. 3.
Chosen projects	

Title:

Purpose:

Goal:

Criteria met:

Title:

Purpose:

Goal:

Criteria met:

Title:

Purpose:

Goal:

Criteria met:

Project criteria:
a. Fit with strategic direction. Match to the vision, mission, and goals.
b. Improving customer satisfaction levels.
c. Improving poor performance trend. Applying best practice.
d. Low-hanging fruit. Relatively easy to accomplish.

Appendix F
STOP Process Worksheets

Process Worksheet 1

Name:	Title:

Your functions:

Your major goals:

1.

2.

3

4.

5.

6.

Tasks you do:	Action
A1.	
A2.	
A3.	
A4.	
A5.	
A6.	
A7.	
A8.	
A9.	
A10.	

Action options: Keep. Eliminate. Combine. Simplify.

Process Worksheet 2

Tasks you delegate:	Action
B1.	
B2.	
B3.	
B4.	
B5.	
B6.	
B7.	
B8.	
B9.	
Meetings you attend:	**Action**
C1.	
C2.	
C3.	
C4.	
C5.	
C6.	
C7.	
C8.	
C9.	

Action options: Keep. Eliminate. Combine. Simplify.

Process Worksheet 3

Reports you write:	Action
D1.	
D2.	
D3.	
D4.	
D5.	
D6.	
D7.	
D8.	
D9.	
Reports you receive:	**Action**
E1.	
E2.	
E3.	
E4.	
E5.	
E6.	
E7.	
E8.	
E9.	

Action options: Keep. Eliminate. Combine. Simplify.

Appendix G
Team Charter

Team Charter

Project title		
Sponsor:	Leader:	Members:
Project goal		
Deliverables		
Key performance measures		
Boundaries		

Critical dates	Start	30-day review	60-day review	Finish

Appendix H
Team Meeting Checklist

Team Meeting Checklist				
Plan	*Project*			
	Meeting purpose			
	Objectives			
	Agenda	Prepared		Published
	Date			
	Time			
	Place			
Run				
	Start time			
	Objective posted			
	Agenda agreed			
	Parking lot set up			
Finish				
	Agreements			
	Action items • listed • assigned			
Follow-up				
	Meeting summary			
	Next meeting	Date	Time	Place
	Action list follow-up			
Team		*Meeting number*		

Appendix I

Meeting Agenda Worksheet

Meeting Agenda Worksheet		
Team:	*Meeting number:*	
Date:	Time:	Place:
Attendees:		
Meeting purpose:		
Objectives: 1. 2. 3. 4.		

Agenda item:	Led by:	Time:
1.		
2.		
3.		
4.		
5.		
6.		
7.		
8.		
9.		
10.		

Appendix J

Team Meeting Report and Action Items List

Team Meeting Report and Action Items List		
Team:		*Meeting number:*
Date:	Time:	Place:
Attendees:		
Summary:		
Action item		

What and how	When	Who
1.		
2.		
3.		
4.		
5.		
6.		
7.		
8.		
9.		

Appendix K

Business Diagnostic Checklist

Business Diagnostic Checklist		
Vision for business:		
Key performance measures: 1. 2. 3. 4. 5.	Target	Actual
Mission for department:		
Key goals: 1. 2. 3.	Target	Actual
Customer needs:		
Major products or services: 1. 2. 3. 4. 5.	Target share	Actual share
Lost sales (reasons customers do not buy): 1. Product 2. Pricing 3. Availability 4. Delivery 5. Quality 6. Other		
Gained sales (reasons customers do buy): 1. 2. 3. 4.		

Business Diagnostic Checklist		
Business performance:	Target	Actual
Financial indicators: 1. Revenue 2. Profit 3. Cash flow 4. Unit cost 5. Other		
Major expenditures (list categories): 1. 2. 3. 4. 5.		
Cost of quality: 1. Prevention 2. Appraisal 3. Internal failure 4. External failure		
General quality measures: 1. Scrap 2. Complaints 3. Warranties		
Production process measures: 1. First-time yield 2. Throughput 3. Productivity		
Distribution process measures: 1. Inventory turn rate 2. Total inventory 3. Transportation cost 4. Storage cost		
Time-based measures: 1. Order to delivery cycle 2. Invoice to cash cycle 3. New product development cycle 4. Asset utilization time 5. Value-added time as a percent of total time		

Appendix L
Training Review Checklist

Training Review Checklist			
Safety:	**Yes**	**No**	**Date**
1. Does every employee know the safety aspects of his or her job?			
2. Is a safety rule book published and distributed to everyone?			
3. Does every employee understand what personal protective equipment he or she is expected to wear?			
4. Are OSHA requirements available, reviewed, and complied with?			
Task:			
1. Has everyone been trained in the tasks they are expected to accomplish?			
2. Have tests been conducted to verify competence?			
Product knowledge:			
1. Is there a basic product training session so that everyone understands the product and service offering?			
2. Is there advanced product training for those who need it?			
Production and service processes:			
1. Does everyone understand how his or her work fits in the overall production and service process?			
2. In the office area, do people understand the basic cash-flow cycle and how their activities can affect it?			
Customers needs:			
1. Does the workforce know who its customers are?			
2. Are customers' needs documented and available to those who supply products and services?			
3. Does everyone understand the basic concepts of internal and external customers?			
Management and supervisory skills:			
1. Has time management been taught to the managers and supervisors?			
2. Do the managers and supervisors know the basics of handling and motivating people?			
3. Has basic project management been taught?			

Bibliography

Ansoff, H. Igor. *The New Corporate Strategy.* New York: John Wiley & Sons, 1988.

Collins English Dictionary. London: Collins, 2000.

Crosby, Philip B. *The Eternally Successful Organization: The Art of Corporate Wellness.* New York: McGraw-Hill, 1988.

Deming, W. Edwards. *Out of the Crisis.* Cambridge: MIT, 1982.

Hale, Roger L., Douglas R. Hoelscher, and Ronald E.Kowal. *Quest for Quality: How One Company Put Theory to Work.* Minneapolis: Tennant Company, 1987.

Hammer, Michael, and James Champy. *Reengineering the Corporation.* New York: Harper Business, 1991.

Herzberg, Frederick. *Work and the Nature of Man.* New York: New American Library, 1978.

Hicks, John. *Comprehensive Chemistry,* 2nd ed. New York: Macmillan, 1970.

Ishikawa, Kaoru. *What Is Total Quality Control?: The Japanese Way.* New Jersey: Prentice Hall, 1985.

Juran, Joseph M. *Managerial Breakthrough.* New York: McGraw-Hill, 1964.

Kiersey, David, and Marilyn Bates. *Please Understand Me: Character and Temperament Types.* Del Mar, CA: Prometheus Nemesis Book Co., 1984.

Labovitz, George H., and Yu Sang Chang. "Learn from the Best," *Quality Progress* (May 1990): 81–85.

Maslow, Abraham H. *Motivation and Personality.* New York: Harper and Row, 1970.

Oakland, John S. *Total Quality Management.* Oxford, England: Heinemann, 1989.

Pande, Peter S., Robert P. Neuman, and Roland R. Cavanagh. *The Six Sigma Way Team Fieldbook: An Implementation Guide for Process Improvement Teams.* New York: McGraw-Hill, 2000.

Peters, Thomas J. "System + Passion + Persistence = Quality Revolution." TomPeters!Company (www.tompeters.com).

Peters, Thomas J., and Robert H. Waterman. *In Search of Excellence: Lessons from America's Best-Run Companies.* New York: Warner Books, 1988.

Robert, Michel. *The Power of Strategic Thinking: Lock in Markets, Lock out Competitors.* New York: McGraw-Hill Trade, 1999.

Roberts, Wess. *Leadership Secrets of Attila the Hun.* New York: Warner Books, 1987.

Shores, A. Richard. *Survival of the Fittest.* Milwaukee: ASQC Quality Press, 1988.

Wall, Stephen J., and S. Charles Zeynel. "The Senior Manager's Role in Quality Improvement," *Quality Progress* (January 1991): 66–68.

Womack, James P., Daniel T. Jones, and Daniel Roos. *The Machine That Changed the World: The Story of Lean Production.* New York: HarperCollins, 1991.

Zook, Chris, with James Allen. *Profit from the Core: Growth Strategy in an Era of Turbulence.* Boston: Harvard Business School Press, 2001.

Index